THE SKEPTIC'S WALK

DENIS DIDEROT

1747

TRANSLATED BY

KIRK WATSON

2018

Table of Contents

TRANSLATOR'S INTRODUCTION - 3 -
PRELIMINARY DISCOURSE - 5 -
THE ALLEY OF THORNS - 18 -
THE ALLEY OF CHESTNUT TREES. - 58 -
THE ALLEY OF FLOWERS - 92 -
KEY TO THE SKEPTIC'S WALK - 118 -

TRANSLATOR'S INTRODUCTION

Even though the *Parlement* of Paris had issued a ruling against Diderot for his first (anonymously published) book, *Philosophical Thoughts* in 1746, Diderot's follow-up was no less radical or provocative.

This is a *Divine Comedy* or *Pilgrim's Progress* for the post-religious age. It is a straightforward allegory about the choice everyone faces in their lives: will you focus on religion, philosophy, or more worldly pursuits? In the path of religion, everyone must walk blindfolded and keep their white robe spotless. In the path of philosophy all is peaceable, but the walk can be chilly. In the path of pleasure and worldly pursuits, life is pleasant for a while, but ennui lurks behind every flower.

In addition to the pleasures of Diderot's digressive, plain, and yet graceful prose, there are additional payoffs for the reader. Diderot packs in several pages of criticism of the historicity of Jesus Christ and the Bible generally, along with amusing attacks on different philosophical systems, including pantheism and atheism, until he concludes by narrating the adventures of misguided lovers and social climbers.

Having condemned his first book to a public burning in the previous year, the authorities managed this time to censor him prior to publication: the autograph copy was stolen by a policeman and placed into safekeeping. In spite of repeated efforts to recover the manuscript, Diderot never saw it again; it first appeared in print in 1830, half a century after his death and 83 years after he wrote it.

So, enjoy a little-known classic. As Diderot says in these pages, even "if you are not amused, you may still benefit from it."

PRELIMINARY DISCOURSE

Those who claim expertise in identifying writers based on literary style, will never find me out. I am no well-known writer. It was random chance that placed a pen in my hand; fame brings too many disadvantages for me fall into the habit of writing very much in the future. I'll tell you the reason why I have consented to write this one time.

Called by birth and rank to the profession of arms, I pursued it, in spite of my natural inclination for philosophy and literature. I was in the war of 1745, and I'm proud of it; I was severely wounded at the battle of Fontenoy; I have seen wars, I have watched as my king encouraged his general by his presence; this spirit passed down to the officers; the officers kept up the bravery of the soldiers; the Dutch were subdued, the Austrians were repulsed, the English were dispersed, and my nation was victorious.

Upon returning from Fontenoy, I retired far away in the country for the remainder of the Fall in a secluded area. I had hoped to evade any visitors, attending strictly to my regime of recuperation; but the company I keep was not made to live unknown, or to be neglected: it's the curse of our state. As soon as I was known to be residing at C..., the whole countryside came to see me. It felt like persecution, and I was no longer able to be alone.

But you, my dear Cleobulus, my worthy and respectable friend, you alone stayed away. I think I was visited by everyone in the world, except the one person I needed most. But how can I blame you: why on earth would you abandon the pastimes of your dear solitude, to die of boredom amid the mob of idlers who surrounded me?

Cleobulus has seen the world and has not been impressed; he soon took refuge in a small plot of land which is all that now remains from what was once a massive fortune; there he dwells as a sage, quite happily. "I'm looking at 50 years of life," he once told me. "My passions have diminished and the hundredth part of the income that I needed at 25, now makes me feel like a rich man."

If some stroke of luck should ever land you in Cleobulus's desert, you will see a man who is serious, yet polite; his manner is not fulsome with compliments, but you can count on his sincerity. His conversation is playful without being frivolous; he speaks freely about virtue; but from the tone he takes on the subject, it seems to agree with him. His temperament is nigh godly, for he does what is just, he tells the truth, he loves the good, and he is self-sufficient.

His retreat is accessed via an alley of ancient trees which have never been pruned or tended by any gardener. His house is tasteful, not showy. Its rooms are comfortable rather than spacious; its furnishings are simple, but clean. He has but few books. The hall, adorned with busts of Socrates, Plato, Atticus, and Cicero, leads to an enclosure which is neither forest, nor meadow, nor garden; it is a combination of all tree. He prefers disorder, which always offers novelty, over symmetry, which is immediately comprehended; he would rather have nature reveal herself in every part of his park; and, really, no artifice is visible unless of natural origin. If anything, there does seem to have been touched by the hand of man, it's a sort of star where various paths run together, and in the middle of the enclosure there is a clearing that is less spacious than irregular.

In that spot I have enjoyed the delightful conversations of Cleobulus countless times, and that of the small set of friends drawn there; for his friends they truly are, and he has no fear of losing them. This is his secret in staying close to them: he never expects anyone to think like himself, and he never harasses anyone about their own tastes or opinions. In that place I have seen a Pyrrhonist giving a skeptic a hug, the same skeptic rejoicing in an atheist's victory, an atheist opening his wallet for a deist, a deist offering help to a Spinozist; in a word, all the philosophical schools united and joined by the bonds of friendship. There dwell harmony, the love of truth, truth itself, openness, and peace; never did any self-righteous man, any superstitious man or fundamentalist, let alone any theologian, priest, or monk ever set foot there.

Entranced by the freshness of Cleobulus's conversations and by a certain guiding principle that I noticed in them, I was content to study them attentively, and I soon noticed that the issues he brought up nearly always had analogies to various objects he saw around him.

Within a kind of labyrinth, composed of high hedges cut from tall, bushy firs, he would always tell me about the mistakes of the human mind, the uncertain nature of our knowledge, the frivolity of the natural sciences, and of the vanity of sublime metaphysical speculation.

While seated beside a spring, if a leaf were disconnected from a nearby tree and the breeze carried it to the water's surface, where the crystal stream would be agitated and its clarity disturbed, he would speak of the inconstancy of our affects, the fragility of our virtues, the power of our passions, the agitations of our mind, the importance and the difficulty in seeing ourselves impartially, and knowing ourselves properly.

Having crested a hill that overlooked the fields and countryside, he inspired me with hatred for everything that elevates man without improving him; he showed me that there was still a thousand times more space above my head than there was below my feet, and he humbled me with respect to the rapidly shrinking portion I occupied in the universe, revealing its fearsome full extent to me.

Returning to the hollow of a valley, he considered the miseries that accompany the human condition, advising me to recognize them without worrying, and to endure them manfully.

Here, a flower reminded him of a light thought or a delicate feeling. There, at the foot of an ancient oak, or in the depths of a cave, he found a muscular and sound argument, a strong idea, or some deep thought.

I understand that Cleobulus styled himself as a kind of local philosopher; that all the region was agitated and talking about him; that every new object lent him novel thoughts of a particular kind, and that the works of nature were, in his eyes, an allegorical book in which he could read any number of truths that escaped the rest of mankind.

To be certain of my discovery, one day I led him to the previously mentioned star. I recalled that in this place I had been struck by the idea that mankind takes so many diverse routes on the way to their ending point, and I wondered whether this place was not similarly heading that way. He didn't disappoint me here: how many important and new truths did I then ignore! In less than two hours that we spent walking from the alley of thorns to the alley of the chestnuts, and from thence to the flowerbed, he emphasized the extravagance of the religions, the uncertainty of the philosophical systems, and of the vanity of worldly pleasures. I took my leave, satisfied that he was right, musing on the clarity of his vision and the vastness of his knowledge; upon returning home, I had nothing better to do than to write down his words, which was easy for me since, to help me understand all the better, Cleobulus had made an effort to speak to me using the vocabulary and imagery of my own art.

Without a doubt, in passing through my pen, these ideas will have lost some of the energy and vivacity they had when first spoken; but I will at least have preserved the main lines of his thought. This is what I now give the world under the title *The Skeptic's Walk: Discussions on Religion, Philosophy, and Worldly Affairs*.

I had already shared a few copies around; they were duplicated, and I have seen the work so monstrously disfigured in some copies that, fearing that Cleobulus, upon discovering my indiscretion, might get the idea that I meant to publish it far and wide, I went to prevent this, to seek his favor, and maybe even obtain permission to publish his thoughts. I was afraid to tell him the purpose of my visit; but I remembered the inscription he had fixed above the entrance to his hallway: *BEATUS QUI MORIENS FEFELLIT* ("Happy are they who die unnoticed") in black marble, and lost hope in the prospects of my negotiation; but he reassured me, he took me by the hand, led me under some chestnut trees, and said: "I don't fault you for seeking to enlighten mankind; that is the most important service that we can offer, but it is also the one thing they will never accept: 'To give the truth to certain people,' as one of our friends once quipped in this very shade, 'is like shining a ray of light on an owl's nest. All it does is hurt their eyes and makes them screech.' If men were ignorant only for lack of learning, perhaps they could be instructed, but their stupefaction is instinctive. My dear Aristos, you're not reaching out to people who know nothing, but to people who wish to know nothing. There are some few whom can awaken, who are in error unwillingly; but how can we reach those who are suspicious even of common sense? Do not expect your work to do much good; rather, be on guard lest it do some infinite harm to you. Religion and government are taboo subjects, not to be discussed. Those who hold the tiller of Church and State would be quite upset should they be compelled to justify the silence they impose on us; however, it is safest to obey and keep silent, at least until we can conjure up some safe haven beyond their reach, from whence we can speak the truth to them."

I responded: “I do see the wisdom in your advice; but without committing myself to follow it, do I dare to ask you why religion and politics are taboo subjects for us? If truth and justice have nothing to fear from examination, it is ridiculous to keep me from inquiring. If I explain myself openly on religion, am I harming it any more than would be done by keeping me silent? If the famous lawyer Cochin, after establishing his case, were to go along with a ruling that his side had no right to pursue its arguments, what would he show he thinks about his rights? The spirit of intolerance reigns among Muslims; their religion is maintained by means of fire and steel—which defeat all arguments; but, as for those who claim to follow and imitate the Master who brought a law of love, goodwill and peace to this world, they try to protect it by force of arms: this is intolerable. Have they perhaps forgotten His biting reprimand to his impetuous disciples when they asked him to call down fire from heaven on those cities which they had failed to convert? In sum, when rational arguments are sound, you can't beat them; when they are weak, you have nothing to fear.”

“One might reply,” said Cleobulus, “that there are certain prejudices which must be kept alive among the populace.”

“And what would these be?” I retorted furiously: “when someone accepts the reality of a God, the reality of good and evil in morality, the immortality of the soul, and future rewards and punishments, what is prejudice good for? Is anyone imbued with the mysteries of transubstantiation, consubstantiation, the Trinity, the hypostatic union, predestination, the Incarnation and all the rest, made a better citizen for all that? If he knows, far better than the most capable professor at the Sorbonne, whether the Three Divine Persons are three distinct and different substances, whether the Son and the Holy Spirit are omnipotent in themselves or subordinate to God the Father, whether the unity of the Three Persons consists in the intimate and mutual knowledge they have of their thoughts and designs, whether there are in fact no Persons in the Godhead, whether the Father, Son and Holy Ghost are only three attributes of the deity—his goodness, wisdom and power, whether these are three acts of His will—creation, redemption and grace, whether these are two acts or two attributes of the Father—His self-knowledge, by which the Son is conceived, and His love toward the Son, which produces the Holy Spirit, whether these are three relations of a single substance, putatively uncreated, engendered and produced, or whether these are three denominations, I ask: Will any of that make this person any more honest? No, my dear Cleobulus, he will conceive all the secret virtues of the *personality*, the *consubstantiality*, of the *homoousios* and the *hypostasis*, but he may be no less a rogue. Christ said: Love God with all your heart, and your neighbor as yourself: this is the law and the prophets. He was too clever and fair-minded to make the virtue and salvation of mankind depend on meaningless words. Cleobulus, it is not for the great truths that the world has been inundated in blood. People only ever kill each other for things that they don't understand at all. Search the history of the Church and you will be convinced that if the Christian religion had retained its original simplicity, requiring only the knowledge of God and love of neighbor; that if Christianity had not been trammeled with an infinity of

superstitions that rendered it, in the ages to come, unworthy of a God in the judgment of the wise; in sum, if it had been preached as a religion whose first beginnings are already present in the soul, it would never have met with any resistance, and those who embraced it would not have been set on each other in disputation. Greed engenders the priests, the priests engender prejudice, prejudice brings wars, and wars last as long as prejudices continue, prejudices as long as there are priests, and priests as long as greed shall exist."

Cleobulus said, "it's like I'm in the age of Paul, in Ephesus, hearing the priests everywhere repeating those accusations that were constantly bringing against him. "f this man is right', the relic merchants cry, 'the end of our trade has come, we must close our workshops and die of hunger!' Aristos, if you believe what I'm saying, you would stifle this thunderclap, put away your manuscript, and only share it with our friends. If they're satisfied with your abilities as a stylist and thinker, they will necessarily give you all due praise. But if, hoping for a wider reputation, the esteem and sincere praise of a small society of philosophers being insufficient for you, then go ahead and produce a book that you may claim as your own. Write a book that you'll be able to sign your name on. Find another subject: you'll find thousands that will lend themselves, even more than this subject, to the sprightliness of your pen."

"As far as I'm concerned, Cleobulus," I told him, I would rather look at what is around me, and I only see two things that are worth paying any attention to, and they are exactly what you forbid me speaking about. Impose silence about religion and the government, and I will

have nothing to say. Really, what do I care if academic *A* wrote a boring novel; if Father *B* delivered an academic discourse from the pulpit; that some Lord *C* inundated us with terrible pamphlets; that duchess *D* seeks favor for her pages; if the son of duke *E* is a bastard or not; if some famous man *F* writes his own books or pays someone else to do it? All such nonsense is inconsequential. They don't touch your welfare or mine. Novelist G's terrible story may be, impossible though it may seem, even four times worse, but the State will be no better or worse. Oh, dear Cleobulus, please let's find us a more interesting subject, or let's take a break."

"My wish," replied Cleobulus, "is for you to enjoy your peace as long as you want it. Write nothing at all if writing may cause you to lose something; but if you truly feel the need to sacrifice your peace of mind to the public, why not just imitate that new writer Denesle, who has got all worked up about prejudices?"

"I hear you, Cleobulus; what you're saying," I told him, "Is to handle the prejudices of the public in such a way as to imply that I share them too. Is that what you think? And what example do you suggest on this account? When I heard about Denesle's book *The Prejudices of the Public*, I said to myself, 'Great! This is what I've been waiting for. Where can I buy it?' I whispered. 'Go to Giffart's, rue Saint-Jacques,' I was told. 'How can this be?' I responded, again to myself: 'Is some honorable censor courageous enough to risk his pension for the sake of the truth, or is this book so bad that a censor let it through at no risk to himself?' I read it and found that the censor had risked nothing. So, your advice, Cleobulus, is that I should write nothing, or that I should write badly."

"Just that," said Cleobulus. "Better a bad writer living peacefully than a good writer under persecution. 'A sleeping book,' as an otherwise quite extravagant writer once said, 'harms no-one.'"

"I would rather try," I replied, "to write a good book, and escape persecution."

"That would be nice," said Cleobulus. "But a safer way to satisfy your tastes without irritating anyone would be to compose a long historical, dogmatic, and critical dissertation, which nobody will read, and which the superstitious will be excused from refuting. This will give you the honor of standing alongside Jan Hus, Socinus, Zwingli, Luther, and Calvin, and nobody will remember any of your books in a year's time. If you prefer to take up the tone of Bayle, Montaigne, Voltaire, Barclay, Woolston, Swift, or Montesquieu, you risk greater longevity; but this advantage will cost something! My dear Aristos, are you sure you know your audience? You may forget that *homoousios* is a word devoid of meaning, and you will thus be taken for an atheist; now, every atheist is damned, and all of the damned are fair game for burning both here and in the hereafter. After this charitable induction you will be persecuted and pursued. 'Satan is the minister of the wrath of God, and it has never struck these people', said one of our friends, 'that they might not be the ministers of Satan's fury.' The more worldly will amuse themselves at your satirical depictions of their morals; the philosophers will laugh at the ridicule you liberally smear on their views; but the devout do not endure taunts, let me warn you: they take everything seriously, and they would rather suffer a hundred good arguments than a single *bon mot*."

"But could you explain, my dear Cleobulus," I replied, "What theologians have against humor? It is true that nothing is more useful than a properly used joke; it seems to me that nothing is more innocent than a terrible joke. To misuse ridicule is like blowing on ice. The moisture of one's breath disappears of itself, and the crystal regains its sheen. In reality, either these somber types are bad at comedy, they're unaware that the true, the good, and the beautiful are not subject to ridicule, or they have a strong suspicion that they have fewer of these qualities than they would like to admit."

"It is the first, of course," said Cleobulus. "For I can think of nothing less endearing than a joking theologian, except maybe a young soldier who would play the theologian. My dear Aristos, you have status in the world; your name is well-known; you have served with distinction; we have proofs of your judgment; nobody is wiser, nobody denies your presence of mind or your intelligence: for you to become popular, people only have to meet and get to know you. Truly, the reputation of being a good writer will add so little to these advantages that you can do very well without it. Have you given a moment's reflection about all those mediocre writers out there? Do you know that a thousand lowly men, jealous of your deserts, will impatiently wait for you to trip up, so they can tarnish all your qualities without fear? Do not risk satisfying their envy in this terrible fashion. Let them go on admiring you, then whither and keep silent."

We would have carried the conversation further, and

there was every indication that Cleobulus, whose arguments had already shaken my resolve, might have succeeded in suppressing my writerly vanity, and my work (or rather his) would have stayed forever under lock and key, when the young skeptic Alcyphron came forward, offered to referee our dispute, and stated that, since the discussion we had shared on religion, philosophy and the world was presently circulating in manuscript, it was already as good as published. But to stave off all the drawbacks that had Cleobulus on his guard, he added: "I advise you to speak with some subject or other of this philosopher-prince you sometimes see, with his forehead banded in laurels, walking in our paths and resting from his noble deeds in the shade of our chestnut trees: the one you recently heard reprimanding Machiavelli[1]. Take refuge, with your book, in his States, and let the bigots rage."

This advice satisfied my tranquility, my interests and my vices; and I followed it.

The persecution of genius fosters its influence.
Tacitus, *Annals*. IV. 35

[1] I.e., Frederick the Great (1712-86), who offered refuge to several philosophers.

THE ALLEY OF THORNS

As in a Company who have lost themselves in passing through a Wood,
Some take to the Right, and some to the Left,
But are all deluded by one and the same Error;
So it is with Mankind, they, who think you a Fool,
Are no better themselves.
-Horace, *Satires*, Book 2, Satire 3

1.

I will never be suspected of wasting millions from the national treasury chasing gold-dust in Peru, or hunting sables in the Lapland. Those whom Louis sent to test the calculations of the great Newton, and those he sent to calculate out the exact dimensions of our globe, explored the stream of Torno without me; they descended the Amazon without my assistance. Moreover, my dear Aristos, I would not recount for you the perils I faced in the icy countries of the North, or in the burning deserts away South: even less shall the advantages of geography, navigation, astronomy extract, in two or three thousand years, any miracles from my quadrant and the excellence of my lenses. I set myself a nobler goal, a utility that's far closer to home. Namely, to enlighten and perfect human reason by telling you about a walk I once took. Does the wise man have to cross the sea, register each barbarian tribe by name, and observe each of the frenzied instincts of the savage races, before he can instruct the civilized? Anything we may find in our own environment is a suitable object for my observation. The objects that are most familiar to us can be transformed into marvels;

everything depends on how we look at them. If we are distracted, we miss the spectacle: if we see directly and meditatively, we will get to the truth.

2.

You know something about this lowly world of ours: the small town I'm about to describe could be under any meridian you like: the town I have recently examined philosophically, after wasting my time running around it as a geographer. I'll ask you to grant such names to the various people who live there according to their customs and features.

How astonished you would be to live among them! But as this strange nation is made up of several different classes, you may not realize which one you belong to, and I can't help but laugh at you in advance, either from the embarrassment that awaits you for not knowing who you are, or for the shame you must feel when you find yourself lost among the mob of idiots.

3.

This empire has for its executive a Ruler, whose name his subjects more or less agree on; but whose existence is very much in dispute. Nobody has seen him, and those of his favorites who claim to have seen and held conference with him, talk so obscurely about him, and have attributed to him contrarieties so strange that, while one part of the nation exhausts itself inventing systems to explain this enigma, or tearing others to shreds to keep their own views dominant, the other has assumed the role of questioning everything about the Ruler, some even disbelieving everything.

4.

Nevertheless, he is assumed to be infinitely wise, enlightened, and full of tenderness for his subjects; but, as he has resolved to make himself inaccessible, at least for the time being, and since any communication from him would necessarily be distorted in transmission, the means he has used to prescribe laws and to manifest his will are rather dubious. Thus, those who claim to be carrying his will have often been exposed as either delusional or impostors, and one is tempted to believe that this may be true of everyone who ever claims to be his envoy. Two large tomes, full of wonders and ordinances, by turns bizarre and reasonable, contain his will. These books are written in such an uneven manner that it truly seems that he has neglected to vet his secretaries, or that his confidence has often been abused by them. The first volume contains many amazing rules, accompanied by a long succession of wonders that confirm them. The second volume revokes the first privileges, while establishing new ones that are supported by new marvels: from this contrast a contest arises between the volumes. The partisans of the second volume claim they are favored to the exclusion of the original one, which they despise as blind, while the supporters of volume I curse the newcomers as intruders and usurpers. I will develop this when I come to the contents of this double-code. Let us return to the Prince.

5.

He lives, they say, in a bright, magnificent and happy dwelling, and we have descriptions of it, although these accounts differ as much between them as do the very imaginations of those who wrote them down. At any rate, everyone is destined for this dwelling. The court of the Prince is a general *rendezvous* towards which we are ceaselessly drawn; and some claim that we will be rewarded or punished there, according to the good or bad things we did *en route.*

6.

Now, we are all born as soldiers; nothing is stranger than the way we get enlisted, while we are weighed down by such lethargy that none of us can even remember whether awakening or sleeping: two witnesses are placed on either side of us, and the sleeper is asked whether he wants to be enrolled; the witnesses consent for him, sign his application, and *voilá,* a new recruit.

7.

In every military organization, certain signs facilitate mutual recognition among the warrior class; this also makes them liable to the deserter's penalty if they abandon the army without orders or just cause. Thus, among the Romans a letter was tattooed on the newly enrolled, which attached them to the service on pain of death. The same expedient is used with us; it was ordained in the first volume of our Code that all soldiers would be marked on the very part in which their virility consists. However, either our Ruler changed his mind, or the opposite sex, ever inclined to contest our advantages, thinking itself no less apt for the battle as ourselves, filed a complaint; and this abuse was reformed in the second volume. No longer did the boot-tips signify enrolment in the military. The troops now wear petticoats; the army of the Prince became a unified *corps* of heroes and amazons, all dressed up in the same uniform. The Minister of War, charged with designing the uniform, went in for a blindfold and a white robe or cassock. It is the custom of the regiment, and we feel strongly that it is better suited for both sexes, than the previous one: an admirable expedient which at least doubled the number of troops. I will even add here that, to the glory of the female, there are few men who wear the blindfold as well as the women do.

8.

The duties of the soldier boil down to keeping their blindfold in place and keeping their robes spotless. The blindfold grows heavy and wears thin with use. For some it feels like a heavy sheet; for others it is but light gauze, always on the point of being torn away. A stainless robe and two equally thick blindfolds: such a thing has never yet seen. You look like a coward if you let your robe get dirty; if your blindfold is torn off or happens to fall, you're a deserter. As for my own robe, dear friend, I will say nothing. They say that bragging about your robe is to stain it, while at the same time, it is possibly indicative of a stain if you say anything negative about it. As to my own blindfold, I got rid of that thing some time ago.

Maybe that was its own inconsistency, maybe it was my own efforts, but either way it's long gone.

9.

They assure us that our Prince has all possible knowledge; but nothing is more obscure than our Code, which is said to originate with him. While much of what we read in it about the robe is sensible, to the same degree, everything it says about the blindfold seems ridiculous. It is claimed, for example, that when this veil is of good fabric, far from depriving us of sight, one instead sees an infinity of marvelous things through it, which are invisible to the unaided eye; and that one of its properties is to act like a kaleidoscope: to display and multiply an object in many places at once; but this absurdity is fortified by others, in which certain deserters have suspected unintelligent writers of audaciously lending ideas to our Lawgiver, and having inserted into the new Code I all manner of puerilities which have no counterpart in the old one. What will surprise you is that they have added a stipulation that knowing all of these reveries is absolutely necessary if a person wants to be admitted into the palace of our monarch. In which case you may ask, what will become of all those who lived prior to the promulgation of the new Code? By my faith! I'm not sure at all... Those who claim to know the secret say, by way of exculpating the Prince, that he revealed these things, by watch-words, to his previous general officers; but they by no means justify him for reforming the whole soldiery who, now long gone, and who will be quite astonished when they arrive at his court to see themselves so shamefully treated only for ignoring what they couldn't possibly have known.

10.

The army resides in obscure regions. It's vain to claim that the region abounds in all good things; it must be unpleasant there; for even they who recruit us never say anything precise about it, but stick to general terms, fearing to go there themselves, and they only go to it as late as possible.

11.

Three paths go there; the one at left is thought to be the safest one; it is certainly the hardest path. It's a small, long alley that is narrow, steep, and covered with stones and thorns which the travelers hope to avoid. This path is only taken with regret, and its inhabitants are always eager to get out.

12.

The second one is wide, pleasant, and covered with flowers; its slope appears gentle. We naturally feel drawn to it; it cuts the route short, which is by no means an advantage; for, as pleasant as it is, one wants it to stretch onwards for a long time. If the traveler is prudent and careful in this alley, he finds the way uneven, tortuous, and uncertain. It seems steep to him; he will notice pits beneath some of the flowers; he fears to make a false step; he leaves it ruefully; he returns to it as soon as he's forgotten about its pitfalls: everyone forgets themselves sometimes.

13.

To the right is a little somber alley, lined with chestnut trees, sandy, wider than the alley of thorns, less pleasant than the alley of flowers, safer than both of them, but hard to follow all the way, as its sand becomes quite unstable towards the end.

14.

In the alley of thorns one finds hair-shirts, sackcloth, disciplines, masks, collections of pious reveries, mystical trinkets, prescriptions for keeping stains off one's robe, or for taking it off, and endless guidebooks for how to keep one's blindfold firmly in place, which are of no use for any but idiots, among which there is not a single one to be found that's of any use for a sensible person.

15.

The alley of flowers is littered with cards, dice, cash, jewels, accessories, fairy tales, and romance novels: everything here is beds of greenery and nymphs whose charms, whether shunned or used, betray no cruelty.

16.

In the alley of chestnut trees, one will find spheres, globes, telescopes, books, shade, and silence.

17.

Upon waking from the deep sleep during which one was recruited, one finds oneself in the trail of thorns, dressed in a white cassock, head adorned with the blindfold. We realize how uncomfortable it is to walk blindly amid the brambles and nettles. And yet, there are some soldiers who bless Providence at every step for having placed them there, who truly rejoice with each scratch they suffer, who rarely succumb to the temptation of soiling their robes, never lowering or tearing off their blindfolds; who firmly believe that the less clearly they see, the more straight they will walk, and who will one day arrive, certain that the Prince will fully appreciate how little use they have made of their eyes, and the particular care that they have taken with respect to their robes.

18.

If you can believe it, these madmen are happy; they do not regret the loss of an organ they don't value; they see the blindfold as a precious ornament; they would shed the last drop of their blood rather than take it off; they are content to worry about the whiteness of their robes: habitual pain renders them insensible to the thorns, and they walk the alley singing, in honor of the Prince, songs which, although old, are still rather beautiful.

19.

Let us leave them with their prejudices: it would be too risky to take them away; their virtue may well come from their blindness. If we deprived them of their blindfold, who knows whether they would take so much care about their robes? Some who cut a fine figure in the alley of thorns might suffer greatly in the alleys of flowers or chestnut trees; and some of those who shine in either of the latter might be carried to the depths of self-flagellation in the first one.

20.

The paths of this sad trail are full of people who have studied it much, who are proud of their knowledge of it, who show it to passers-by, but who aren't simple-minded enough to walk in it themselves.

21.

In general, this is the most wicked race I know of. Proud, greedy, hypocritical, deceptive, vindictive, but above all quarrelsome, from Rabelais's Friar John (of blessed memory) they learned the secret of beating their enemies with their flag-pole[2]; they would kill each other for mere words if one were kind enough to leave them to their own devices. They have been able, I know not how,

---

[2] I.e., a cross.

to persuade the recruits that they have the exclusive privilege of taking off their robes: this makes them very useful to those people who, with their eyes caked with so much caulk, have no trouble believing that their robes are dirty when they are told so.

22.

These saints ramble and enjoy the day in the alley of thorns and spend the night shamelessly in the alley of flowers. They claim to have read in the laws of the Prince that they are not allowed to have their own wives; but they scrupulously skip over the part about not touching those of other men, so they willingly caress the wives of the travelers. You wouldn't believe how circumspect they have to be about revealing these exploits to their comrades; for they take great care to unmask each other. When they are successful, which often happens, they are piously bemoaned in their alley, while others laugh heartily in the alley of flowers, and we spitefully mock them in our own alley. If their maneuvering steals some subjects away from us, their absurdity brings them back: to the shame of humanity, they have as much and even more to fear from a joke than a rational argument.

23.

To give you an even better idea, I must explain to you how the very large number of these Guides forms a kind of military staff with its superior and subaltern ranks, wages greater or lesser according to varying degrees of dignity, colors and uniforms: these are multiplied almost to infinity.

24.

First there is a vice-regent who, for fear of scraping the soles of his feet, which have become quite soft, has himself carted around in a chariot, or carried in a sedan chair. He politely calls himself the Humble Servant of all, but he patiently allows his satellites to maintain that everyone is in actual fact *his* rightful slave; and, by dint of repetition, they get the imbeciles to believe this nonsense: that is, quite a few people. We do find, in some cantons of the alley of thorns, certain recruits whose blindfold begins to wear out, and who begin to question the despotism of the vice-regent. Against him they bring out old parchments containing the orders of the assembly of the Estates-general; but in each response he begins by writing to them to tell them that they're wrong; then he agrees on a single word, and if the rebels reject him, he withholds their pay, their instruments of labor, cuts off their pension, and often gives them very saucy slaps indeed—such matadors have sometimes been whipped like naughty children. He possesses, at their expense, a very fine estate, the main exports of which are vellum and soap, for he is the premier degreaser in to the world, in virtue of an exclusive privilege which he exercises quite graciously, for a fee. His first predecessors dragged themselves on foot through the alley of thorns; many of their descendants are lost in the alley of flowers. Some of them walk beneath our chestnut trees.

25.

Under the headship of a man like that, whom you might take for Don Japheth of Armenia, so easily infatuated he is with all he sees, and he piles hats upon hats, you find governors and sub-governors of provinces: some thin and gaunt, others beaming and ruddy, some agile and brave. They make up an order of chivalry distinguished by its long cane of crow's beak, and by a headgear borrowed from the officiants at the cult of Cybele, whom they otherwise do not resemble at all; they have given proofs in this regard. They qualify themselves as the Prince's lieutenants, and the vice-regent calls them his servants. They also have a soap-store, but it is less fine and consequently less expensive than that of the vice-regent, and they have the secret of a balm as marvelous as that of brave Fierabras[3].

26.

After these comes a numerous body of officers spread out in many geographical posts, to whom, like Turkish *Sipahis*, who are accorded a *timar* or a province which is more or less opulent: that is, most of them go about on foot, some on horseback, and a small number by coach. Their function is to show the new recruits the ropes, to recruit even more soldiers, to comfort the novices with speeches on the necessity of bearing the blindfold with grace and keeping their robes spotless—which are, ironically, the very two things they neglect in their own lives, since they're apparently too busy mending the

[3] A balm that healed whoever drank it.

blindfolds and scrubbing the robes of their neighbors; for these are still more of their duties.

27.

I almost forgot to mention a small, distinguished troop outfitted with bullfinch caps and catskin mantles. These take themselves to be the defenders of the title and rights of the Prince, and most of them don't even believe in his existence. Some time ago, an important post in their number became vacant. Three competitors fought over it: an imbecile, a coward, and a deserter; sorry, I mean an ignoramus, a libertine, and an atheist; the deserter prevailed. They amuse themselves by disputing in barbarous terms about the Code which they interpret according to whim, which is obviously a favorite pastime of theirs. If you can believe it, one of their colonels has even claimed that, when the son of the Prince performs the general enumeration of the subjects of his Father, he may as easily come in the form of a calf as that of a man. The elders of this troop drool with such expertise as to lead one to believe they have been practicing it their whole lives. The blindfolds begin to chafe at the younger ones; they have no more than linen left, some have nothing at all. They walk about quite freely in the alley of flowers and mix with us under the chestnut trees, but furtively, in the dark.

28.

Finally, we have the auxiliary troops, under command of very rich colonels. These are a kind of marauder, making a living from the spoils they can get off of those who walk the alley. It is said that most of them once skillfully leeched off those whom they led to the posts of the garrison, one to a château, another to a farm, this one to a wood, that one to a pond, and that by this means they amassed these ample lodgings they possess between the alley of thorns and that of flowers. Some old ones either hold out their hands, going from door to door, or simply rob the passers-by. These vile troops are divided into regiments, each having its own standard, its bizarre uniform, and its even stranger laws. Don't expect me to describe the different segments of their armor... almost all of them have for a helmet a kind of mobile window, or sugar-loaf's crust, which now covers their head, now falls on their shoulders. They have retained the mustache from the Saracens and the boots from the Romans. It is from one such body that, in certain cantons of the alley of thorns, the great provosts, the archers, and the executioners of the army find their origins. This war council is ruthless: any travelers who refuse to wear the blindfold must be burned alive, along with those who do not wear it to their tastes, and any deserters who cast it off; but this is done out of charity. It is from this one, and above all from a great dark battalion, where the swarms of recruiters come from, who claim to be commissioned by the Prince, to beat the drum in foreign lands, to make recruits in other countries, and to persuade the subjects of other rulers to discard the coat, the cockade, the cap, and the blindfold they received from their rulers, and put on the uniform of the alley of thorns. When these recruiters themselves are caught, they are hung, unless they themselves turn deserter; and they usually prefer to desert than to be hung.

29.

But not all are so enterprising; some forego adventures in distant and barbarous lands. Inhabitants of a smaller hemisphere, these ones follow different vocations, according to their own talents and the guidance of their leaders, who use them skillfully for the benefit of their corps. Those whom nature has favored with a good memory, a fine voice, and helping of audacity, incessantly cry to all passers-by that they are making missteps, will never show them the right way, and will be well-paid for his views, however all his merit amounts to repeating what a thousand others, equally misinformed like himself, have already said. Those with some mental agility, the gift of gab, and a scheming mind will get themselves set up in a sort of box, where they'll spend half their lives listening to secrets that are rarely amusing and mostly false, but always lucrative. Moodiness and sadness frequently take hold of these poor souls. We have nevertheless often seen betrayed love set itself up there in ambush, to leap on novice hearts, and draw young pilgrims into the alley of flowers, under pretext of showing them how to walk more comfortably in the trail of thorns. There, everything is revealed: secrets, fortunes, affairs, gallantries, plots, jealousies. All is used gainfully, and the consultations are rarely given free of charge. Those who lack imagination and genius will instead take up numerology or spend all their time transcribing the thoughts of others. Others will use the power of observation to figure out, from rust on a bronze object, the origins of a city which has been forgotten for a thousand years or more, or wear himself out for ten years toiling, successfully, to make an idiot of a spoiled brat. There are some who handle brushes, spades, files or planes, but many others have embraced the calling of layabouts who boast of their own importance. He, who knows these latter, fears or avoids them; there are many who think they know them, but few really know their hearts.

30.

The confidence and eagerness of the people for the enclosed-ones is astounding. They boast of possessing a panacea; the prescription consists in telling a jealous husband that his wife isn't a flirt, or that he must love this flirt just as she is; to a loose woman, that she should hold onto her sixty-something husband; to a minister, that he should have more integrity; to a merchant, that it is wrong to charge usury; to an unbeliever, that he would do well to believe; and so on like this. "Do you want to be healed?" said the doctor to the sick man. "Yes, I do," he responded. "Move along then, you are healed." The good people depart fully satisfied, and it may be true that, in fact, they are better off.

31.

It is not long since among the Guides arose a large sect of ascetics who frightened the travelers by teaching that the robes had to be extremely white, and went along crying in the houses, in the temples, in the streets, and on the roofs that the tiniest spot is an ineradicable stain; that the soap of the vice-regent and the governors was worthless; that they should righteously take from the stores of the Prince, and soak in his tears, which he gave *gratis*, but in very small quantities, and that nobody who wanted them had any. In addition, as if there were not already enough thorns in the path, these maniacs scattered caltrops and *chevaux de frise* which render it impassible. The travelers lose hope; it's only cries and groans all around. With the impossibility of following such a punishing route, the masses were on the point of crossing into the alley of flowers or coming to stroll under our chestnut trees when the dark battalion invented down slippers and velvet mittens. This expedient prevented mass desertions.

32.

Here and there one finds great aviaries in which birds—all of them female—are shut up. Here devout parrots chatter affectionate speeches, chirping in a jargon they do not understand; there, the young doves sigh while mourning the loss of their liberty; elsewhere, fluttering and deafening in their cackling, dwell some linnets whom the Guides enjoy whistling at through the bars of the cage. Those among these Guides or *strolling serinettes*, who are old habitués of the alley of flowers, remind them of lily-of-the-valley and of roses. What torments these captives most of all is being able to hear the passersby but being unable to follow or mingle with them. However, their cages are spacious, clean, and well stocked with millet and sweets.

33.

You must know the army and its leaders well enough by now: let us pass on to the military Code.

34.

It is a sort of mosaic, carried out by a few hundred different workers who added patched it together bit by bit according to whim: judge for yourself whether the brew turned out right.

35.

This Code is composed of two volumes; the first was begun around year 45,317 in the Chinese calendar, thanks to the efforts of an old shepherd who knew very well how to use a double-ended baton, and was a great conjurer to boot, as he would demonstrate so well to the lord of his parish, who did not want either lower his taxes, or exempt him from drudgery, neither him nor his family. Pursued by the archers, he left the canton and took refuge with a farmer whose sheep he then tended for forty years, in a desert where he practiced his magic tricks. He claimed, on the sole faith in his own integrity, that one day he saw our Prince without actually seeing him, and that he received the title of lieutenant-general from him, along with the staff of the commander. Armed with this authority, he returned to his country, gathered his family and friends, and exhorted them to follow him to a country which he said had belonged to their ancestors (and indeed they had once passed through the region). Then our rebels gathered together, and their leader declared his plans to the lord of the manor. The lord refused to let them leave and treated them as upstarts. At that instant the old shepherd murmured a few words between his teeth and the baron's ponds were suddenly poisoned. The next day he cast a spell on the sheep and horses. Another day he gave the lord, along with all his people, scabies and diarrhea. After several other attacks, he ended up killing the lord's first-born and all the other eldest children in the city with anthrax. Ultimately, the lord consented to let him go: they departed, but only after having stripped his château bare and pillaged the rest of the citizenry. The gentleman, bothered by this last move, mounted a horse and chased them, at the head of his servants. But, our bandits had already forded a river; happier still for them, their erstwhile master, being unaware of the real situation, tried to cross it a little lower down and drowned with almost all his people.

36.

Before gaining the town to which their leader had lured them, they wandered in the desert where the conjurer kept them so long that they all ended up dead. During this interval he relieved his boredom by writing a history for his nation and composing the first part of the code.

37.

Its history is based entirely on stories that grandparents repeated to children at the fireplace, based in turn on their memories of the verbal narrations they learned from their own grandparents, and so on, back to the beginning. Quite a way to preserve a true history!

38.

It tells of how our ruler, after establishing the seat of his empire, took a little silt, blew on it, animated it, and thus made the first soldier; how the woman he gave to him once made a bad dinner, thereby imprinting a black stain on their children and their furthest descendants, which made them odious to the Prince; how the regiment was augmented; how the soldiers became so wicked that the monarch had them all drowned, except for one barracks whose leader was a rather good man; how the children of this man repopulated the world and scattered over the surface of the Earth: how our Prince, who was no respecter of persons, nevertheless chose a select few to be his people, and how he made this people from a woman who was beyond the age of childbearing, along with an old man who was still green enough to sleep with the occasional servant-girl. Here is the precise origin of the first privileges, as mentioned above, and after this follows the detail of their generations and their adventures.

39.

It was said of one, for example, that the ruler commanded him to cut his own son's throat, and that the father was about to follow through when a footman appeared, announcing clemency to the innocent victim; of another, that his governor found him, while watering his horse, a gorgeous mistress; of this one, that he fooled his father-in-law twice over, after having tricked his own father and his elder brother, that he slept with both sisters and then with their chambermaids, and another one, with his daughter-in-law; of another, that he struck it rich by figuring out riddles, and made his family opulent in the lands of a lord whose steward he was; of nearly all of them, that they had fine dreams, saw the stars at midnight, were susceptible to seeing ghosts, and bravely fought against goblins. What wonderful stories did the old shepherd pass on to posterity!

40.

As for the Code, here are its main points. I have already mentioned that the black stain had already made the Prince hate us. Guess what he demanded by way of recovering his favors which had been lost in such a strange manner? Something stranger still: all the children must have a certain quantity of their flesh removed, an operation I have already mentioned, and they were annually condemned, as a family, to eat a pancake without butter or salt, with a salad of dandelions without oil. Another fee, payable weekly, was to walk for a whole day with your arms tied behind your back. An order was that each must provide him or herself with a blindfold and a white robe, and to wash it, on penalty of death, in the blood of the lamb and pure water: you see that the origin of the blindfolds and white robes is quite ancient. To this purpose, the regiment included companies of butchers and carriers of water. Ten little lines of text contain all the orders of the Prince; the Guide of our fugitives published it and closed it up in a rosewood case, which, as oracles go, was not outdone by the tripod of the Sibyl of Delphi. The rest is a heap of arbitrary rules about the proper manufacture of tunics and mantles, how to dine properly, the regulation of wines, the knowledge of meats, both easy and hard to digest, the appointed times for walking, sleeping, and certain other things that might happen in the absence of sleep.

41.

The old shepherd, assisted by one of his brothers, whom he furnished with a great income which became a family inheritance, wanted to subject, by harsh means, his companions to all these regulations. Immediately there arose murmuring, unauthorized gatherings, questioning of his authority, which he would have easily lost if he had failed to destroy the rebels by digging a mine under the land they were on. This event was seen as a heavenly vengeance, and the miracle-worker didn't disabuse anyone of this suspicion.

42.

After many other adventures they drew near to the country which they were to take possession of. The leader, who did not want to make any binding promises to his subjects, and who loved war, but only from his armchair, went on to die of hunger in a cavern, after having strongly encouraged them to have no mercy on their enemies, and to be great usurers, two commissions which they followed amazingly well.

43.

I will not carry on describing their conquests, or the establishment of their new empire and its various revolutions. You will have to read the book, in which you will see (if you can) the historians, poets, musicians, storytellers and all the town criers proclaiming the coming of the Son of our monarch and the reformation of the Code.

44.

He actually did appear, not with a carriage and a train worthy of his birth; but like those adventurers we often see establishing or conquering empires with only a handful of brave and determined men; that was once in fashion. For a long time, his fellows thought he was a man like any other, but one fine day they were astonished to hear him giving a speech in which he arrogated the title of the son of the ruler, along with the power to abrogate the old Code, with the exception of ten lines thereof, and to substitute another in its place. He was simple in morals and speech. He renewed, on pain of death, the use of the blindfold and the white robe. He prescribed very praiseworthy things about the robe, more difficult still to practice, but he retailed in strange statements about the blindfold. I have already told you some of these; here are others. For example, he expected that, when one had their eyes well covered, they should see as clear as day; that the Prince his father, himself, and a third personage who was at the same time his father and son, being so perfectly mixed together that they only form a single and unique whole. You might think he was old Geryon returned to earth. You must forgive me for using a fable to explain this miracle. Unfortunately, you do not know about *circumincession*—you have never been informed of this marvelous dance, where the three Princes shimmy around each other to all eternity. He added that he would be a great lord one day, and that his ambassadors would offer an open table. Prophecy was fulfilled. The first ones graced with this title did hold great dinners and drank his health generously; but their successors economized in this regard. They discovered, somehow, that their master had a secret way of folding himself under a single crumb of bread, and getting himself swallowed whole, in a single instant, by a million of his friends, without causing any of them the least indigestion: this in spite of the fact that, in reality, he stood five feet six inches tall, and they ordained that the supper would be converted into a breakfast, to be eaten without any beverage. Some freethinking soldiers murmured about this. They proffered insults and came to blows: much blood was shed; by this division, which brought others along with it, the alley of thorns was reduced to half of its population, and nearly lost the whole thing. I give you this as an example of the kind of peace that the new lawgiver brought to the kingdom of his father, and I pass over other ideas lightly; they have been taken down in the minutes by his secretaries, the two main ones of whom were a fishmonger and a cobbler, who was once a gentleman.

45.

The latter, a babbler by nature, retailed in amazing stories about the excellence and the marvelous effects of an invisible staff which the Prince distributes, he said, to all his friends. It would take volumes to tell you, even succinctly, what these Guides have conjectured since then, and written self-assuredly, and how they have gnashed and torn into each other about the nature, power, and properties of this staff. Some have claimed that without it is impossible to take one step; others, that it was perfectly useless, provided that one has a good pair of legs and strong desire to walk; these, either rigid or supple, short or long, proportional to the capacity of the hand and the difficulty of the route, and that would have been lost except by his fault; those, which the Prince owed to none, refused to many, and often retracted from those to whom he had given it previously. All these opinions were based on a great treatise on staffs, composed by an old professor of rhetoric, to serve as a commentary to a chapter by the fishmonger on the importance of crutches.

46.

There is another article that has been no less divisive among them: namely, the infinite goodness of our ruler, which this rhetorician has claimed to reconcile his premeditated and irrevocably fixed resolution to eternally exclude from his Court, and to cast into the dungeons, without hope of reprieve, anyone who was not enrolled in his service: innumerable peoples who haven't so much as heard of him, many others whom he judged unworthy of his favor, or who were out of his favor because of their ancestor's rebellion; casting fortunes by toss of a coin, as it were, he will favor others who are quite guilty. This Guide sensed the full absurdity of his ideas. Thus, God knows how, in his own case, he escapes the terrible difficulties that he has raised. When it gets really murky, and he gets lost, he cries *Careful about the potholes!* and all those who likewise attribute caprice and barbarity to our Prince, repeating with him: *Careful about the potholes!* All these things and a thousand others of the same kind are seen as respectable in the alley of thorns. Those who walk there consider them true, and even agree that if any were false, all must likewise be false.

47.

However, the defenders of the old Code rose against the son of the Prince, demanding he show his family tree and credentials. He proudly responded: "My works will prove my origins." A noble response, but inadequate for a Nobleman. However, it was claimed that he did harm to the memory of the Old Shepherd, and under this pretext the companies of butchers and carriers of water, whom he had threatened to replace with fullers and degreasers, formed a conspiracy against him. His treasurer was corrupted; he was taken, condemned to death and, worse still, executed. His friends proclaimed that he died and also that he did not die: that he reappeared at the end of three days; but past experience kept him at the Court of his father; and he has not been seen since. While departing, he charged his friends with collecting his laws, telling everyone about them, and hurrying to put them into practice.

48.

You must understand that the laws, which cannot speak, must be interpreted: it was not different with his laws. Some find them too indulgent; others too rigid; some say they're absurd. As the new corps was formed and extended, it experienced internal divisions and met with external obstacles. The rebels gave no rest to their companions and received none from their mutual enemies. The times, prejudices, education, and a certain stubborn fondness for new and forbidden things increased the number of these enthusiasts, however. They soon went as far as to assemble and mistreat their hosts. They were punished at first as lunatics, then as rioters. But the majority were certain that they paid court to the Prince by getting themselves slaughtered for things they did not understand, braved the shame and the rigors of torture, and factious men and imbeciles were converted into heroes: what amazing effects of the Guides' eloquence! This is how the alley of thorns gradually became populated. In the beginning it was quite deserted; it was long after his death that the Son of our monarch won troops and made some noise in the world.

49.

I have told you so much that you may well conjecture that nobody ever did such great things. But no: be aware that nobody lived or died in greater obscurity. I will soon explain this phenomenon; but first, I would like to share the conversation of an old resident of the alley of chestnut trees, with some of those who planted the alley of thorns. I learned this from a writer who seemed well informed about what went on in those days.

He relates that the dweller of the alley of chestnut trees spoke first to the compatriots of this so-called Son of our ruler, and one of them responded a sect of visionaries had been founded, who took an impostor for the Son and envoy of the Great Spirit: a rebel whom the judges of the province had crucified. He adds that Menippus, which is the name of the dweller of the alley of chestnut trees, immediately began to question those who tended the alley of thorns:

"Yes," they told him, "our leader was crucified as a subversive, but he was a divine man, all of whose actions were miraculous. He exorcised demons; he made the lame walk; he gave sight to the blind; he raised the dead; he himself was also resurrected; he ascended to heaven. A great number of our own have seen him, and the whole country has been a witness of his life and his miracles."

50.

"Really, that sounds fantastic," replied Menippus. "Those who saw so many marvels, no doubt all of them joined up with you: so, have all the residents of the country donned the white cassock and the blindfold?"

"Alas! No," they responded. "The number of those who followed was very small in comparison with the rest. They have had eyes and did not see, had ears but did not hear."

"Ah!" said Menippus, somewhat recovered from his surprise, "I see; I recognize the enchantments, ordinary as they are to those of your nation. But tell me sincerely; did things really happen as you say? Were the amazing deeds of your colonel proclaimed to the world?"

"Have they indeed?" they responded. "News broke out across the face of the whole province. Whatever malady anyone had, they only had to touch the hem of his garment as he walked by, to be healed. On many occasions he fed five or six thousand in audience with what would hardly have sufficed for five or six men. This is not to speak of an infinity of other miracles: once he raised a dead man who was being put in the ground. On another occasion, he resurrected another who had been interred for four days."

51.

"At this last miracle, I am sure, then, that those saw it must have bowed down at his feet of this wondrous man and worshiped him as a God," said Menippus.

"Some did, indeed, believe and join us," they responded, "but not all. Moreover, most of these informed the butchers and carriers of water, their mortal enemies, about what they had seen, and got them riled up against him. His other deeds produced no such effects. If some of those who were witnesses took sides, it was because they were destined, from all eternity, to follow its banners. There is even something strange in his conduct in this regard: he made a point of beating his drum in those places where he knew that nobody had any desire to join us."

52.

"Truly," Menippus responded, "either you're all pretty stupid, or your enemies are morons. I easily see (by your example) that he may have found people idiotic enough to imagine that they were witnessing miracles when they really weren't; but you can't say that they were so stupefied as to dismiss miracles as amazing as those you describe. There is no doubt that your country produces wholly unique sorts of people. You folks can see things that are not visible anywhere else."

53.

Menippus admired the credulity of these fine folks who seemed to be fanatics of the first order. To better satisfy his curiosity, he added in a tone that seemed to disavow his last words: "What I've heard seems so marvelous, strange, and novel that I would take extreme pleasure in knowing everything about your leader. You're making me inform myself about it. Surely the whole world deserves to know about the least actions of such a divine man's life."

54.

Immediately Mark, one of the first pillars of the alley of

thorns, maybe flattering himself that he might recruit Menippus, narrated in detail all the prowess of his colonel, how he was born of a virgin, how the mages and the shepherds recognized his divinity, even when he was in diapers; along with the miracles of his childhood and of his later years. His life, his death, his resurrection: nothing was omitted. Mark did not confine himself to the actions of the Son of Man (as his master sometimes preferred to call himself since there was danger in taking up ostentatious titles); he adduced his speeches, his addresses, and his maxims; the initiation was finally complete, covering both the history and the rules of conduct.

55.

When Mark left off speaking, Menippus, who had listened patiently, without interrupting, began to speak, and continued, but in such a tone as to show him how reluctant he was to augment his recruitment.

"The teaching of your leader," he said, "is indeed pleasing to me. It is in keeping with that which wise men, who appeared on Earth more than four hundred years before him, once taught. You spout them as if they were new, and perhaps they are new to such a stupid and base people; but they are old hat to the rest of us. Nevertheless, they bring to mind a thought that I really must share with you: that it is astonishing that the man who preached them was not more consistent in his acts. I fail to conceive how your colonel, whose ethical thoughts were so good, also performed so many miracles."

56.

"But if his morality says nothing new to me," added Menippus, "I confess that things are different with respect to his miracles: these are a complete novelty to me. But they should not be novelties either for me, or for anyone else. Your colonel hasn't been dead all that long: everyone who is now of their rational age was contemporary with him. Can you say in good faith that, in a province of the Empire that welcomed as many travelers as Judea did, that such extraordinary things could happen for three or four sequential years without anyone hearing about them? We have a governor and a large garrison in Jerusalem; the country is full of Romans; commerce is continual between Rome and Jaffa, and yet nobody was even aware of the existence of your leader. His compatriots were able to see his miracles or not as they pleased; but other men ordinarily see what is before their eyes, and that is all they see. You tell me that our soldiers attested the miracles that happened at his death and his resurrection, and the earthquake, and the thick darkness that blocked the sun for three hours, and all the rest. But when you tell me these people were seized with fear, dismayed, embattled, and collapsed at the sight of a visible intelligence coming down from the sky to lift the stone that sealed his tomb; when you claim that these same soldiers later denied, through some base self-interest, the miracles that had struck them so powerfully, although they had almost died in fright, you forget that they were men, or at least you will metamorphose them into Idumeans, as if the air of your country mesmerized the eyes and blinded the rationality of any foreigner who breathed it. You must accept that, if your leader did the least part of the deeds you attribute to him, the Emperor, Rome, the Senate, and everyone else would have heard about it. This divine man would have been widely discussed and generally admired. However, he is as yet unknown to the masses. The whole province, with the exception of a few residents, took him for an impostor. Consider this, Mark: the greatest miracle of all would have been to suppress all that information about such a public, striking, and marvelous figure as he was. Please recognize your mistake and abandon these illusions; for, ultimately, it's only your imagination that created all the miracles with which you embellish your history!"

57.

Mark remained silent for a while after Menippus's speech; then, taking a fanatical tone, said: "Our leader is the son of the Almighty! He is our Messiah, our Savior, our King! We know that he died and was resurrected. Blessed are those who have seen and believed, but even more blessed are those who believe in him without having seen. Rome, renounce your incredulity. Proud Babylon, hide under sackcloth and ashes; repent! Hurry! The time is short, your fall is near, and your empire is at an end. I say empire, but the whole world is going to be remade; the Son of Man will appear on the clouds and judge the living and the dead. He comes quickly; he is even at the door. Many of those who are alive today will see these things fulfilled."

58.

Menippus, who found this reply distasteful, took leave of the troop, departed from the alley of thorns, and left the fanatics to make as many speeches as they would, in their efforts to populate this alley.

59.

Now, Aristos, what do you think about this discussion? I present it for your consideration. You may say, 'I agree that these Idumeans must be great idiots; but is it impossible that a nation should produce some clever teacher as well? The Thebans, the thickest people in Greece, gave us Epaminondas, Pelopidas, and Pindar, and so I would rather Menippus had interviewed the historian Josephus or the philosopher Philo than the Apostle John or Mark the Evangelist. The majority of imbeciles was always allowed to believe what the minority of intelligent ones couldn't; and the stupid docility of the former never impacted on the enlightened testimony of the latter. Tell me then: what said Philo regarding the colonel of the alley of thorns?' ...Nothing. 'What did Josephus think about him?' ...Nothing. 'What about Justus the Tiberian?' Nothing at all. So, how would you suggest Menippus discuss the life and actions of this man with well-informed persons, when they never heard anything about him? In their writings they forgot neither the Galilean Judas, nor the fanatic Jonathan, nor the rebel Theudas; they are all silent about the Son of your ruler. What about that, then? Did he get lost among the multitude of impostors who continually rose up in Judea, who only had time to make an appearance and then leave the stage?

60.

The residents of the alley of thorns have been deeply struck by the silence of contemporary historians regarding their leader, and more even by the hatred that the ancient residents of the alley of chestnut trees felt for their kind. In this emotional state, what idea did they conceive? To negate the effect by destroying its cause. "How", you will say, "did they destroy the cause? I can hardly follow you. Did they make Josephus speak a few years after his death?" Exactly; you've got it: they inserted into his history a section praising their colonel; but notice their clumsiness; having failed to include any verisimilitude in the morsel they composed, and being unable to find a suitable spot in which to place it, everything about this passage is suspicious. They made Josephus—a Jewish historian, and a pontiff to his nation, a man scrupulously holding to his religious faith, deliver a speech by one of their Guides; and where did they place it? In a spot where it bisects and mutilates his narrative. "But, these impostors did not always understand their own interests," said the author from whom I got the discussion between Menippus and Mark. "By trying to do too much, they lost everything. Two lines, silently insinuated anywhere else, would have done the job with better effect. For example, this Jewish historian, who was no friend of Herod's, detailed his cruelties: here they should have inserted the massacre of the children of Bethlehem, since he says nothing about any such thing."

61.

You may have your own opinion about that: but come back to the alley of thorns with me.

62.

Among those who enter the alley of thorns nowadays, some hold their blindfolds with both hands, as though the blindfolds were resisting and trying to get away. You will recognize the best heads for this purpose: it has always been noted that the blindfold rests best on a narrow and ill-formed forehead. But what comes of the resistance of the blindfold? One of two things. First, either their arms tire and it falls off, or they keep it in place and eventually achieve victory through their efforts. Those whose arms fall will suddenly find themselves in the position of a man born blind whose eyelids were suddenly pried open. Every object in nature appears to them quite differently from what they had heard about them. These illuminated ones cross over to our alley. May they have the pleasure of resting under our chestnut trees and breathing the fresh air with us! How joyous they are to watch the daily healing of the cruel wounds they once gave themselves! How tenderly they mourn the unhappy lot of the wretches they left behind in the alley of thorns! They don't always dare to offer a helping hand to them: afraid that, not having the power to follow through, they themselves may be dragged back again, through their own weight or by the efforts of the Guides, into heavier undergrowth. It never occurs to these refugees to abandon us. They grow old beneath our shade; but, at their point of departure for the general rendezvous, they will run into a great number of Guides; and since people are often rendered imbeciles in their last moments, these Guides take advantage of this condition to replace their blindfold and give their robe a final shake, which they believe is an important service they render. Those of us who are in full possession of their reason prefer not to interfere in this operation, because they have persuaded everyone that it is shameful to appear before the Prince without a blindfold, and without being *washed* and *pressed*. Polite people call this 'finishing the journey decently'; for our age loves decorum.

63.

I have crossed from the alley of thorns into that of the flowers, where I soon felt the shadow of the chestnut trees, which I do not flatter myself I will enjoy all the way to the end of the journey: one can't be certain of anything. For all I know, I may well finish the route with a blindfold in place, like anyone else. However that may be, I am now certain that our Prince is ultimately good, and that he will focus more on my robe than on my blindfold. He knows that we are weaker than we are wicked. Moreover, such is the wisdom of the laws that he has prescribed, that we cannot even disobey them without suffering immediate punishment. If this is true, as I have heard demonstrated in the alley of thorns (for, although those in command there live quite badly, they often have quite good intentions). If it is true, I say, that the degree of our virtue is the precise measure of our current happiness, this monarch might annihilate us, without doing any injustice to any of us. At any rate, I tell you that this thought is not my own; I don't want to be annihilated; I would rather continue to exist, sure as I am that I can only ever be good. I think that our Prince, who is no less wise than he is good, does nothing that will not lead to some good: now, what advantage can he derive from the suffering of a bad soldier? *His own satisfaction*? I am careful not to believe this; it would be an insult to him to think he is more wicked than I am. *For the gratification of the saved?* This would be a feeling of vengeance, incompatible with their virtue, in which our Prince, who is not guided by the whims of others, would take no interest. *We cannot say that he will punish anyone as an example*; for so many executions would leave no man standing. When our rulers inflict punishment, it is because they hope to frighten those who would be otherwise tempted to act like the guilty.

64.

But before leaving the alley of thorns, it is important also that you should know that those who follow it are all subject to a strange vision: they believe they are haunted by an evil magician, as old as the world and a mortal enemy of the Prince and his subjects, who invisibly swirls around their heads, hoping to debauch them, endlessly whispering in their ears that they should drop their walking stick, soil their robe, tear off their blindfold and cross over to the alley of flowers or that of the chestnut trees. When they feel pressed too hard, they make a symbolic gesture with their right hand which sets the magician careening, especially if they have dipped the tip of their finger into a certain water which can only be prepared by the Guides.

65.

I might never finish if I had to go into details on the properties of this water, or the power and the effects of the sign. The history of the magician has led to the creation of thousands of books, all of which show what a fool our Prince is by comparison: that this magician has played a hundred pranks on him, and that he is vastly better at stealing people than his rival is of keeping them. But, for fear of incurring the same censure that was laid on Milton, namely, that this accursed magician became the hero of the story (although some will probably say that he wrote this book himself), I will only say that he is represented with the hideous form that the Duke of Médoc gave to his magician Freston (in his dour sequel to Cervantes's excellent work); and that it's thought that those who listened to him in the alley of thorns, will be abandoned to him the doors of the garrison, to share with him, for all eternity, in the gulfs of flame, the terrifying fate to which he is destined. If that is true, that will be the first time when so many honest men gathered with so many scoundrels, in such an ugly meeting-hall.

THE ALLEY OF CHESTNUT TREES.

Draw near in order, and listen,
While I prove that you are all mad.
Horace, *Satires*, Book 2, Satire 3

1.

The alley of chestnut trees is a pleasant place to stay, and it bears a close resemblance to the ancient Academy. I mentioned that it was dotted with thick groves and somber retreats where silence and peace reign. Those who inhabit this alley are naturally grave and serious, without being taciturn or harsh. Professional disputers, they love conversation and even arguing, but without that bitterness and stubbornness with which their neighbors enjoy yelping about their dreams. Diversity of opinion does nothing to alter the commerce of friendship, and in no way impedes the exercise of virtue. Opponents are attacked without hatred, and although they are pressed mercilessly, victories do not grant any right to vanity. In the sand you can see traces of circles, triangles, and other geometrical figures. Here systems are made, but not much poetry. I think the *Epistle to Uranie*[4] was written in the alley of flowers, somewhere between the Champagne and the Tokay.

[4] A poem by Voltaire (which talks about tearing away the blindfold of prejudice).

2.

Most of the soldiers in this path go on foot. They follow it in secret; and they would complete their voyage peaceably if they were not assailed and disturbed now and again by Guides from the alley of thorns, who consider and treat them as their most dangerous enemies. I warned you that few people are seen there, and you will find even fewer if you only count those who reach the end. Unlike the alley of flowers, it's not wide enough to accommodate many travelers; it's made only for those who can walk without a cane.

3.

An important question is whether this section of the army forms a *corps* and can constitute any kind of society. For there are no temples here, no altars, no sacrifices, or any Guides. No common banner is followed there; no general rules are known: the multitude is split into many bands, and all of them are zealous about their independence. They live like in those ancient governments, where each province would send deputations to the general council, and each had equal powers. You will have solved this problem after I've traced out the main lines of these warriors.

4.

The first company, whose origins stretch very far back

into ancient times, is made up of people who plainly tell you that there is neither alley, nor trees, nor voyagers; that everything visible could just as easily be something or nothing at all. They have, it is said, a marvelous advantage in combat; that of being unburdened of having to cover themselves; all they care about is striking the enemy. They have neither armor, shield, nor cuirass, but only a short sword, with two edges, which they use with utter deftness. They attack everyone, even their own comrades; when they have dealt you wide and deep wounds, or when they are themselves covered with wounds, they suffer with impressive composure, as if it were only a game, saying they have not really wounded you, since they have no actual swords, and you have no bodies; that they might well be mistaken, but that the safest bet, both for them and for you, is to examine very well whether they are really armed, and if this quarrel which you're complaining of, is not actually a sign of their friendship. It is said that their first captain, while walking down the alley, walked in every way possible, often upside down, often backwards; that he would violently run into the passers-by and the trees, falling in holes, sprain himself, and when someone offered to guide him, he responded that he had not moved from his initial spot, and that he was getting along very well. In conversation, he maintained the *pro* as well as the *contra* indifferently—first he would establish an opinion, then he would demolish it; he would caress you with one hand, then slap you with the other one, and finished each time by saying: "Did I really hit you?" This troop would have had no standard, except that after about two hundred years one of their champions came up with a design. It's a set of balancing scales embroidered in gold, silver, wool and silk, with this motto: *What do I know?*

His fantasies, written in a disorganized manner, haven't failed to make converts. These soldiers are good for ambushes and stratagems.

5.

Another cohort, no less ancient, although less numerous, is made up of deserters from the previous one. They affirm that they do exist, and that there is an alley, and that the trees are real, but they claim that the ideas of regimentation and garrison are absurd, and even that the Prince is but an illusion, that the flag is the livery of idiots, and that the fear of immediate punishment is the only argument for keeping stains off your robe. They boldly stride towards the end of the alley, where they expect the sand to melt under their feet, where they will be swallowed up, no longer holding on to anything, no longer being held by anything.

6.

The next group thinks quite differently. Certain of the existence of the garrison, they believe that the Prince, in his infinite wisdom, has not left them without lights, and that reason is a gift they received from him, and which is adequate to regulate their march; that they must respect the Ruler, and that they will be either well or ill received by him, according to what they did on the journey; that his severity will not be excessive, or his punishments beyond limits; that, upon arrival at the rendezvous, nobody will leave ever again. They submit to social norms, they know and cultivate the virtues, detesting crime, and see well-tempered passions as necessary for their happiness. Their gentle temperaments, they are abhorred by those of the alley of thorns. Why, do you ask? Because they have no blindfold; they say that two functioning eyes are all they need to get around; they must be convinced by sound reasons whether the military Code is truly the workmanship of the Prince, since they find much in it that is incompatible with their ideas of his wisdom and his goodness.

"Our ruler," they say, "is too just to disapprove of curiosity: What is the goal of our searching, if not to know his will? We have been shown a letter from him, and we have all his workmanship before our eyes. When we compare the two, we can't see how such a great artisan could also be such a bad writer. Is this contradiction not striking enough that we ought to be forgiven for noticing it?"

7.

A fourth band will tell you that the alley is carved out on the back of our monarch, a fantasy that's even more absurd than the dreams about the Atlas of the ancient poets. He held up the sky on his shoulders, and fiction embellished an error. Here, reason and some dubious expressions are toyed with to imply that the Prince forms part of the visible world, that the universe and he are one and the same thing, and that we ourselves are part of his vast body. The leader of these visionaries was a kind of partisan who made frequent incursions, and often caused great concerns, in the alley of thorns.

8.

Beside these march, irregularly and in a disorderly fashion, even stranger champions: each of these maintains that they are alone in the world. They only believe in the existence of a single being; this thinking being is they, themselves: since everything that happens within us is only impressions, they deny that anything else exists; thus, they are all simultaneously the lover and the mistress, the father and the child, the bed of flowers and he who tramples on it. I recently met one who assured me that he was Virgil.

"How happy you must be," I said, "to have been immortalized by the divine *Aeneid*!"

"Who? Me?" He asked. "I am no happier than you are."

"What an idea!" I replied. "If you are the Latin poet (and it may as well be you as anyone else), you will agree that you are infinitely worthy for having imagined so many great things. What a burning fire! What harmony! What style! What fine descriptions! What fine order!"

"What do you mean, order?" he broke in: "There is no shadow of any such thing in the work in question: it is only a tissue of ideas that don't mean anything, and if I had to congratulate myself for the eleven years I spent stitching together ten thousand verses, it would be about giving myself, in passing, good compliments about my skill in subjecting my fellow-citizens through proscriptions, and honoring myself with the names of father and defender of the fatherland, after having been its tyrant."

My eyes grew wide at all this rigmarole, and I did my best to reconcile such disparate ideas. My Virgil noticed that he had confused me.

"You have a hard time understanding me," he continued. "Okay, I was at the same time Virgil and Augustus, Augustus and Cinna. But this isn't all; today I am whoever I want to be, and I will show you that maybe I am you, and that you are nothing; *if I rise to the clouds, or descend to the abyss, I will not stop being myself, and it is never anything but my own thought that I perceive,*" he was telling me emphatically, when he was interrupted by a noisy troop which single-handedly caused the whole tumult that was heard in our alley.

9.

These were young, crazy kids who, after having walked so long in the alley of flowers, would often come with their heads still spinning into ours; they were all bedazzled, and they might have been thought drunk, the way they looked and talked. They cried that there was no Prince or garrison, and that at the end of the alley they would be all joyously annihilated; but for each of these fancies not a single sound proof was offered, not one logical demonstration. Like those who go by night singing in the streets, to make others believe and maybe convince themselves that they have no fear, they try to make a great racket. If they came back from this thundering for a few moments, it was to hear the words of others, to catch a few scraps, and repeat them as if they made them up themselves, while adding a few off-color stories to them.

10.

These boasters are detested by the wise among us, and well deserve to be: they have not disciplined any of their footsteps; they are continually going from one alley to another and back again. They drift into the alley of thorns when gout strikes them: it has no sooner passed when they launch into the alley of flowers, until the *tocane* draws them to us; but the effect is short-lived. Soon they go on and abjure everything they said to us at the feet of the Guides, all the time being apt to get out of their clutches at the earliest opportunity, as soon as the pungency of the remedies carries new aromas to their heads. *Their state of health, for better or worse, is the substance of their whole philosophy.*

11.

While I was contemplating these falsely brave men, my visionary friend slipped away, and I was amused to consider others who laughed at all the travelers, having no opinions of their own, and thinking that none can be taken as reasonable. They know not where they come from, why they are here, or where they are going, and they care little about these things; their battle-cry is: *All is vanity.*

12.

Among these troops, some from time to time go in detachments to make little skirmishes, and draw, if they can, deserters or prisoners: the alley of thorns is the site of their incursions; they slip in furtively by means of a procession, a wood, a fog, or some other stratagem suited to the secret of their march, and they fall on the blind ones they find, scatter their Guides, distribute manifestos against the Prince or satires against the vice-regent, steal their staffs, tear off the blindfolds and then slip away. You would be tempted to laugh when you see the surviving blind men without their staffs, unsure where to set their feet or what path to take, they walk about blindly, go astray, cry, losing hope, begging for someone to help them back on the path, while wandering further astray with every step: the uncertainty of their feet leads them further and further from the wide alley where habit leads them.

13.

When the authors of this disorder are captured, the war council treats them as brigands and vagabonds, without a commission by any foreign power: which is very different from how we behave. Under our chestnut trees we listen calmly to the leaders of the alley of thorns; we wait for their attack, we fight back, we dismay them, we confound them, where possible, we enlighten them; we bemoan their blindness, at least. Patience and peace regulate our behavior; theirs is dictated by rage. We use reason; they gather kindling. They preach love but breathe blood. Their language is humane, but their hearts are cruel. No doubt about it: the reason they think of the Ruler as a tyrant is to justify their own bloodlust.

14.

Some time ago I overheard a conversation between a resident of the alley of thorns and one of our comrades. The former, always wandering with his eyes covered, came to an enclosure of greenery in which the other was dreaming. They were only separated by a lively hedge, thick enough to keep them apart, but not enough to obstruct their voices. Our comrade, after many arguments had been laid out, cried aloud, as happens with those who think they are alone:

"No, there is no Prince; there is no clear evidence of his existence."

The blind man who heard was confused, and he took the speaker for one of his own comrades, whispering to him: "Brother, have I taken a misstep? Am I not well inside the alley? Do you think we have still a long way to go?"

15.

"Alas!" replied the other, "unfortunate fool, you are tearing and bloodying yourself in vain: a poor dupe of the dreaming of your leaders, go and walk as far as you like, but you will never arrive at the promised destination, but if you are not in love with these rags, you will see, as we do, that nothing is more ill-conceived than that tissue of nonsense that they lull you with.

Only, tell me, why do you believe in the Prince? Is your belief the fruit of your own meditation and intelligence, or is it only prejudice and listening to your leaders? You agree with them and you see nothing at all, and then you boldly pronounce strong opinions about everything. But you should begin by examination, weighing arguments, if you want a more sensible judgment. May I have the pleasure of pulling you out of this labyrinth where you're going astray? Come here, let me have your blindfold."

"By the Prince, I will do no such thing," responded the blind man while recoiling three steps and raising his guard. "What could I say for myself; what would become of me, if I arrived without my blindfold, with my eyes wide open? But we can talk, if you like. Maybe you will disabuse me of my illusions; as for me, I think I can bring you to my side. If I succeed, we'll walk together; after sharing the dangers of the route, we will likewise share the pleasures of the great rendezvous. Begin, I'm listening."

16.

"Right then", replied the resident of the alley of chestnut trees, "to start with, you have roamed for thirty years with a thousand anxieties on this cursed avenue: tell me, are you any further along now than you were on the very first day? By now, you must be able to see, more clearly than before, the doorway, some apartment, or a pavilion of the palace where your Ruler lives. Do you see some path to his throne? No: forever distant from him, you will never come any closer. So, you must agree with me that you entered into this path without any solid foundation, with no impulsion other than the similarly unfounded example of your family, your friends, and your neighbors, none of whom has brought any genuine news from that fine country where you expect to retire someday. If a businessman took the advice of an impostor or ignoramus and, in search of treasure, left home and braved a thousand perils, crossing stormy and unknown seas and parched deserts, in a land he only knew from the conjectures of another traveler no less mistaken or ignorant than himself, would you not refer this man to the nearest insane asylum? You are this businessman. You follow, through brambles that tear your skin, an unknown route. You have no idea what you're looking for; instead of seeking to enlighten yourself along the way, as a rule you walk unguided, with your eyes blindfolded. But, tell me, if your Prince is reasonable, wise and kind, how can he be happy for you to dwell in such profound darkness? If this Prince ever appeared to you, how would you recognize him through the darkness you shroud yourself in? How will you distinguish him from a usurper? And what do you want him to think about your unkempt appearance—contempt or pity? And, if he doesn't exist, what good are all these wounds? If you had any sensations after death, you would be eternally consumed by remorse for participating in your own destruction during the short time that was given to you to enjoy your existence, and for imagining your ruler so cruel as to feast on blood, cries and horrors."

17.

"Horrors?" cried the blind man in a rage. "The only

horrors are the ones coming out of your mouth, you wretch. How can you dare to question and even deny the existence of the Prince? Why can't everything, both inside and outside yourself, convince you? The universe shouts it to your eyes, reason to your mind, and crime to your heart. I agree, I do hope for a treasure I have never seen; but where are you going, eh? Off to annihilation? What a fine end to aspire to! You have no reason for hope; your lot is fear, and this leads to despair. What does it matter if I get scraped up for half a century while you were having fun, if, when you appear before the Prince without blindfold, robe, or rod, he sends you off to tortures infinitely more brutal and insufferable that the passing discomforts I've been through? I risk little to gain much; and you risk nothing at peril of losing all."

18.

"Easy now, friend", replied the dweller of the alley of chestnut trees. "You're presupposing what's in question: the existence of the Prince and his court, the requirement of a particular uniform, and the importance of keeping blindfold in place and keeping your tunic spotless. But allow me to deny all these things to your face; if they are false, the consequences you draw from them will fall of their own accord. But if matter is eternal, and if movement alone could arrange and imprint it originally with all the forms that we see preserved in it, what need do have I for your Prince?

"There is no general rendezvous, if what you call the soul is really just an after-effect of our physical organization. As long as the economy of our organs lasts, we are able to think; we become irrational when it suffers alteration. When it is annihilated, what becomes of the soul? Moreover, on what do you base your idea that, when detached from the body, it will keep on thinking, imagining, and feeling? But let's talk about your rules: based on arbitrary conventions, they are the product of the original Guides and not of reason, which, being common to all humanity, has always indicated the same route, prescribed the same duties, and forbidden the same actions to everyone, for why would it favor them with greater knowledge of certain speculative truths than with knowledge of moral truths? Now, everyone unanimously agrees on the certainty of the former: as for the latter, from the banks of one river to the next, from this side of the mountain to the other one, from this border to that one, by crossing a geometrical line, things change from white to black. So, start by dissipating these clouds, if you want me to see clearly."

19.

"Quite happily", replied the blind man. "But I must sometimes rely on the authority of our Code. Do you know it? It is divine. It teaches nothing that is not based on facts superior to natural forces, and consequently on proofs incomparably more convincing than those which reason could provide."

20.

"Oh no, don't bring your Code into it", said the philosopher. "Let's have a fair fight. I've come in good faith, without armor, but you want to cover yourself with a heavy outfit better suited to discomfort and crush its wearer than to protect him. I would be ashamed to fight you in that condition. What do you think about it, then? And where did you get the idea that your Code was divine? Does anyone honestly believe it, even in your own alley? And one of your leaders, on pretext of attacking Horace and Virgil... need I go on? I despise your Guides too much to use their authority against you. How can the fantastic stories that fill this book possibly benefit you? How can you believe, how can you make others believe in such amazing things on the mere word of writers dead for over two thousand years, while your contemporaries constantly lie to you about events that are closer to hand, and which you can easily check for yourself! You yourself, in a story you constantly retell about something you know first-hand, and in which you're interested, will embellish it a bit, take out a few things, and continually change it; such that some of your narrations could be compared against others, and it would be impossible to decide between your contradictory judgments; but you boast that you are reading with utmost precision in the obscurity of past ages, and easily reconciling the dubious narrations coming from your first guides. Truly, this is to respect them more than you do yourself, and by no means do you ever allow your self-respect to get a word in."

21.

"Ah! What monster did you just conjure?" replied the blind man. "He is the author of the stains you see on our robes; he is, within you, the germ of this presumption which prevents you from bridling your reason. Ah! If you knew how to tame him like we do! Do you see this hair-shirt and this cilice? Wouldn't you like to try them on? This is the discipline of a great servant of the Prince: let me hit you a few times, for the good of your soul. If you only knew the sweetness of these mortifications! How much good they do a good soldier! How, by the *purgative* life, they lead on to the *illuminative* life, and then to the *unitive* life. What a fool I am! I'm speak to you in the heroes' language; but now, to punish myself for having profaned it and given you the gift of understanding..."

22.

At that very instant, the cords began to swing and the blood flowed. "Wretch!" His opponent cried out: "Are you insane? If I were less nice, I'd laugh at the ridiculous figure you cut. I can only see you as a blind hospital patient who would tear his own shoulders to restore the sight of one of that eye-doctor Gendron's pupils, or Sancho thrashing himself to break Dulcinea's enchantment. But you are a man, and so am I. Stop it, my friend; your self-respect, which you think is tamed by this barbaric technique, is actually benefited by it, and doubles up under your discipline. Stop swinging your arm and listen to me. Can you really honor the vice-regent by disfiguring his portraits? And if you thought so, would the satellites of the war-council not seize you at once, and would you not be cast into a dungeon for the rest of your days? On to the application: you see that I am arguing according your own rules. The external signs of veneration for princes have no basis other than to flatter their pride, and perhaps the true misery of their condition, which must needs be hidden from them. But your prince is supremely happy. If he is sufficient unto himself, as you yourself say, then what good are your vows, your prayers, and your contortions? He either already knows what you desire, or he is completely ignorant of it; if he knows it, he is determined to give it to you, or to withhold it. Your pleading will not rip any gifts from his unwilling hands, and your cries will not hasten them along."

23.

"Ah! Now I see now who you are", replied the blind man. "Your system would ruin a million proud edifices, break open the doors of our aviaries, convert our guides into laborers or soldiers, and bankrupt Rome, Ancona, and Compostella: from which I conclude that it is destructive of all society."

24.

"But that's the wrong conclusion," replied our friend. "It is destructive only of abuses. We have seen great societies subsisting without this paraphernalia, and there are still some lucky enough to be ignorant even of the names of such things. Setting these peoples on a parallel with those who boast of knowing your Prince, and properly examining the falsehood or the contradictions in the ideas that these boasters express, you will infer more soundly that he does not exist. For, take note, would you ever have known your father if he always stayed in Cuzco, while you were living in Madrid, and he had only ever given you a few dubious signs of his existence?”

25.

"But what should I have thought about him," the blind man continued, "if he had left me in charge of some portion of his inheritance? You must agree that the Great Spirit gave me the ability to think, to reason. I think, therefore I am. I did not grant existence to myself. It came from another, and this other is the Prince.”

26.

“This is a clear sign, then”, chortled the stroller of the alley of chestnut trees, “that your father has disinherited you. But this reason, of which you boast so highly, how do you use it? In your hands it’s a useless instrument. As long as you remain under the guardianship of your guides, it only drives you to despair. It shows you in their speeches, which you take for oracles, a capricious ruler, whose good graces you vainly think can be secured through your perseverance in overcoming these thorns and dodging these stones and potholes. For example, do you know whether he hasn't actually decided that your patience will fail at the very end of the alley, and you will raise the corner of your blindfold from curiosity, and soil your robe, even a little? If he has pre-determined this to happen, you will succumb and find yourself lost...”

27.

“Oh, no,” said the other, “The wonderful rewards that await me will buoy me up.”

“But what do these wonderful rewards consist of?”

“Of what? Of beholding the Prince; of seeing him once again; of seeing him forever and being always so enraptured by this sight, as if seeing him for the first time.”

“And how so?"

“How? by means of a dim lantern that will be embedded in the pineal gland, or on the corpus callosum, I'm not sure which, which will show us everything so clearly that....”

28.

“All in good time”, said our comrade. “But for now, it seems to me that your lantern is terribly smoky: all your words show that you serve your master only from fear, and that your attachment to him is based on self-interest; this base passion is only for slaves. So, take a second look at this self-regard, against with you declaim so angrily; it becomes the only motive for your actions; and now you want your Prince to crown it. Go on, you’ll gain no less by joining us: freed from fear and greed, you will at least live in tranquility, and if you risked anything, at most this would be ceasing to exist, at the end of your career.”

29.

"Stooge of Satan!" replied the blind man. "*Vade retro*[5]! I can now see that all the strongest arguments pass over your head. Wait a minute; I will get some better weapons."

30.

He suddenly began to scream, "Blasphemer! Deserter!" And I saw furious guides come running from all sides, with kindling under their arms and torches blazing. Our partisan hid himself quietly in the alley, which he rejoined by some indirect trails. Meanwhile the blind man, having taken up his staff, and following his alley, related his adventure to his comrades, who pressed close to congratulate him; after much praise, it was decided that they would print their arguments under the title of: *The Physical and Moral Science of the Existence and Properties of Light, by a Blind Spaniard, Translated and Ornamented with Commentaries and Scholia by the Wardens of the Ophthalmological Hospital 'The Quinze-vingt'*. Everyone who thinks they see clearly without knowing why, for the past forty years or more, is invited to read it. But, as for anyone who fails to find a copy, you will be pleased to know that it contains nothing more than the preceding conversation, only inflated and revised to give the bookseller enough pages for a properly-sized volume.

---

[5] Translator: "Get behind me."

31.

The noise that this scene had caused reached the ultimate confines of our alley, and it was judged appropriate to gain clarity on the facts of the matter and to call a general assembly where the validity of the arguments that the blind man and Atheos (this was our friend's name) could be debated. Everyone who knew about their dispute was summoned to depict its character, but without weakening or giving a ridiculous turn to the arguments. I had been seen near the battlefield, and while I felt some repugnance exposing the weaknesses of a badly-supported cause, and I keenly felt my duty to truth. Our champion repeated his objections and I repeated the replies of the blind man with complete fidelity; it was found that we were unanimous in our reaction, as is usual among us. Some said that only weak arguments had been used on the other side; others that the beginning of the dispute might produce *advantageous clarifications* useful for the common cause.

The friends of Atheos won and promised nothing less than to subjugate the other companies one by one. My own comrades and I maintained that they were doing the victory dance before the action had begun and that, since they'd pulverized a few bad arguments, they shouldn't get too uppity lest some good ones came their way. In this conflict of opinions, one of our number proposed we form a detachment of two men from each company, to send ahead in the alley and to stipulate, with regard to whatever was discovered later, who would be the colonel from then on, and what ensign we should use.

This seemed like sound advice, and we followed it. From the first band we chose Zenocles and Damis; from the second Atheos, or the hero from the adventure with the blind man, along with Xanthus; Philoxenus and myself were deputed from our band; the fourth sent Oribasius and Alcmeon; and the fifth chose Diphilos and Nerestor; elections were held in the sixth; and all its members mingled equally in the ranks; when it was insisted by all that we should allow none among the army's pikes whose morality, constancy, ignorance, or faithfulness was in question...they did obey, but they complained. We took for our watch-word *the truth*, and we set off. The army corps camped to give us time to get ahead of it, and set its pace by our movements.

32.

It began on one of those fine nights that a novelist wouldn't let escape without first extracting the tribute of an ample description from it. I, who am only a historian, will only say that the moon was at its zenith, the sky cloudless, and the stars very bright. I chanced to end up beside Atheos, and we were walking, at first in silence, but then I couldn't bear going on for so long in silence. I spoke first, addressing my neighbor thus: "Do you see," I asked, "the brilliance of these stars; the regular course of some, the immobility of the others, the way they support each other, their usefulness for our own globe? Where would we be without these torches? What generous hand lit all of them and deigns to maintain their light? We have enjoyment of them; will we be so ignorant as to attribute their production to mere chance? Won't their existence and their amazing order lead us to the discovery of their author?"

33.

"All of that leads nowhere, my dear friend," he replied. "You see this illumination with the eyes of some kind of fanatic. Your imagination, rising to this pitch, reshapes the light into a pretty decoration, for which it then pays honor to some being or other who never had anything to do with it. This is the same presumption as that of a yokel who enters the city, watches Servandoni's *Armide*, and thinks that he designed the gardens and the Sun Palace just for him. We have before us an unknown machine, on which observations have been made which prove the regularity of its movements, according to some, and its disorderliness, according to others. An ignoramus, never having studied anything more complex than a simple gear, will notice a few of its teeth, then extrapolate that these must be enmeshed within a hundred thousand other gears and springs whose interplay he doesn't understand, and finishes like an artisan, by placing the inventor's name on the assembled piece of work. —"But," I responded, "let's pursue the comparison further: doesn't a balancing pendulum, a repeating clock, not reveal the intelligence of the watchmaker who constructed them, and would you dare say that they are produced by chance alone?"

34.

"Be careful," he replied. "The two things are not analogous. You compare a finished piece of work, whose origin and designer are known, to an infinite compound, whose beginnings, present state, and end are unknown, and whose author is only conjectural."

35.

"But why does it matter," I replied, "when it began, or by whom it was made? Do I not see what it is? Does its structure not cry out for an engineer?"

36.

"No," replied Atheos: "you don't know what it is. How sure are you that the order which you so admire here does not become disorder somewhere further down the line? Are you sure that you can extrapolate from one point to all of infinite space? We fill a vast land with hills and piles of terrain, rubble-heaps formed at random, but inside these the worms and ants find very comfortable habitations. What if these insects were to react as you do, and wax ecstatic about the intelligence of the gardener who designed such a bountiful world for their benefit?"

37.

"Neither of you understand at all, gentlemen," Alcmeon cut in. "My colleague Oribasius will show you how the great luminous orb, which will appear soon, is the eye of our Prince; that these other radiant points are either the diamonds of his crown or the buttons on his cloak, this evening he is wearing an opaque blue. You entertain yourselves arguing about how he dresses; tomorrow he may change: maybe his great eye will be full of emotion, and his robe, today so shiny, will be dirty and grubby: how will you then recognize him? Oh! Look inside yourselves instead. You are part of his being; he is in you and you in him. His substance is unique, immense, and universal; only it exists: the rest is only modes thereof."

38.

Philoxenus cut in: "To hear you talking like that, your Prince is a strange compound: he cries and laughs, sleeps and wakes, walks and rests, is happy and unhappy, sad and gay, is impassive and yet suffers; he experiences the most contradictory states and affections all at once. He is, in one and the same being, both an honest man and a rogue, both wise and idiotic, teetotal and debauched, soft and cruel: he joins all the vices and virtues together; I cannot imagine how you keep all these contradictions straight."

Damis and Nerestor joined with Philoxenus against Alcmeon and took turns explaining to each other; they added argument to argument, first against the ideas of Alcmeon, then those of Philoxenus, and finally turned to the conversation I'd had with Atheos, and ended by responding pensively to us: "We shall see."

39.

But night gave way to day, and as the sun began to appear we discovered a quite large river which seemed to cut our alley short with its various bends. Its waters were clear, but also deep and swift, and none of us wanted to risk a crossing. We sent Philoxenus and Diphilus to find out whether there was a shallower section ahead, where we might ford it. The rest of the troop sat down near the stream on a patch of grass in the shade of willows and poplars. We saw, further along, a chain of steep, pine-covered mountains.

"Do you not thank your Prince," asked Atheos ironically, "for having, created for your welfare, two things that now enrage so many good people: a river which nobody would dare cross for fear of drowning, and beyond them those mountains where we'll certainly die of exhaustion or hunger? A sensible man who plants a garden for the benefit of himself and his friends would not include features like these. You say that the universe is the work of your monarch; at least you agree that these two portions betray his bad taste. What could this watery affluence possibly be good for? A few streams would be enough to keep these plains green and blooming, and what about these massive heaps of boulders—do you really think they're better than a nice prairie? Once again, all of this owes its existence less to rational design than to the jesting of a madman."

40.

"But what would you think," said I, "of a regional official who, having been absent from his Prince's council and never having much information about his plans, started to complain about a certain tax, the marching or the idleness of the armies, the placement of the fleets, and attributed the success of some negotiation or a sea-expedition to chance alone? No doubt you would be ashamed of his error; but you're making the same one. You condemn the positioning of this river and these mountains because they rub you the wrong way at this moment; but are you alone in the universe? Have you weighed each of these objects against the good of the whole system? Do you know for sure that this body of water is not required to fertilize other climates that you know nothing about? Might it not provide an important commercial link between several great cities on its banks? What good would your milder streams do if a dry and sunny spell dried them up? These mountains that hurt your eyes now are covered with plants and trees of established utility. We extract minerals and metals from their bowels. On their tops are immense reservoirs fed by rain, fogs, snows and dews, and from which waters are distributed economically, forming distant streams, springs and rivers. These, my friend, at the intentions of the Prince. Reason has placed you within reach of his mind, and you're clever enough to see that an immortal hand dug these reservoirs out and cut these canals."

41.

Zenocles, who had been observing this dispute, became anxious and gave us a gesture, as if asking us to lay down our weapons. He said, "it appears that both of you are going so quickly. Look, according to you, a river and mountains, right? As for me, I maintain that what you call a river is in fact a solid crystal on which we can walk without any peril, and what you call mountains are in fact nothing but a vapor, thick but permeable. Watch, I'll show you."

At that moment he leaped into the river and sunk more than six feet down. We all feared for his life; fortunately, Oribasius, a good swimmer, jumped in after him, caught onto his cloak and brought him to the shore. Our anxiety was replaced by bursts of laughter at the hilarious state he was in. But he, opening his eyes wide and completely dripping wet, asked us why we were so cheery, and how we'd been.

42.

Meanwhile, our scouts returned in a hurry. They told us that by following the river a long way they had found a natural bridge in the form of a huge boulder, under which the waters had carved out a passage. We crossed the river and descended around three miles, skirting the mountains and leaving the river to our left. Zenocles often wanted to rush straight up into the heights to our right, as he said, just to pierce that fog.

43.

We finally arrived at a cheerful valley that divided the mountain range and bordered a vast plain covered with fruit trees, but mostly by mulberry bushes whose leaves were covered with silkworms. We heard the droning of swarms of bees in the hollows of several trees. These insects labored endlessly, and, as we carefully contemplated this scene, Philoxenus used the occasion to ask Atheos if he thought that these industrious animals were mere automatons.

44.

“If I were to argue,” said Atheos, “that they are all little magicians, some wrapped in the rings of a caterpillar, others in the body of a fly, as one of our friends once did, you would listen to me: if not with pleasure, at least without anger, and you would speak to me better than anyone ever did in the alley of thorns.”

45.

“You have spoken well”, Philoxenus replied humbly. “I can't darken such light and innocent banter with odious hues. Far be it from us to have the spirit of persecution, which is against both graciousness and reason; but taking these insects as anything but complex machines, made by one who knows how to make them so skillfully...”

“I can see where you're leading," interrupted Atheos. "And that is your Prince? What a fine picture; your great monarch in the sky, practicing his technique on the legs of a caterpillar and the wings of a fly!”

46.

Filled with contempt, Philoxenus replied: "That which captures our admiration as men may likewise deserve the attention of the Creator. In the universe nothing is made or put in place without some purpose..."

"Oh! Always with your purposes!" continued Atheos. "We can no longer believe in such a thing."

"These gentlemen are the confidants of the Great Artisan," added Damis, "but, like scholars commenting on writers, they end up making them say things that were not in the original text."

47.

"No, absolutely not!" continued Philoxenus. "Since, with the aid of the microscope it has been discovered that silkworms have heads, hearts, intestines, and lungs; the mechanism and the functions of these parts have been discovered; the movements and filtrations of the fluids that circulate in them has been studied, and the work of these insects has been examined, are people only talking about chance, in your view? Setting aside the industriousness of bees, I think that even the very structure of their proboscises and stingers presents to every intelligent mind such marvels that it never inclines to believe that these could ever be the production of some extremely fortuitous motions of matter."

"These gentlemen," interjected Oribasius, "have never read Virgil, one of our patriarchs, who claims that the bees received a portion of the rays of Divinity, and that they form part of the Great Spirit."

"Both you and your poet have yet to consider," I replied, "that you divinize not only flies, but every drop of water, and all the grains of sand in the sea: what absurd pretensions. Let us return to those of Philoxenus. If his careful observations of some insect are decisive as to the existence of our Prince, what greater advantage will we not gain from studying the anatomy of the human body and the knowledge of other phenomena of nature?"

"Nothing more," Atheos kept repeating, "than the fact that matter is organized."

The rest of the company, witnessing his difficulty, told him by way of consolation that, while he may in fact be right, yet probability favored my position.

48.

"If Philoxenus has the upper hand, it's Atheos' fault," Oribasius quickly replied. "He only had to take a further step to win definitively. 'Nothing follows from Philoxenus's words,' he had said, 'except that matter is organized; but if we can demonstrate that matter, and even its organization, are eternal, what becomes of Philoxenus's speech?' He could have added."

49.

"If there were never any being, there never would be one," Oribasius continued gravely. "Since, to grant existence to oneself, one must act, and to act, existence is necessary."

50.

"If there had only ever been material beings, there would never have been intelligent beings, for either intelligent beings gave themselves existence, or they must have received it from material beings; if they gave themselves existence, they would have acted before they existed; if they received it from matter, they would be its effects, and from this I find them reduced to the quality of modes, which is far from what Philoxenus is saying...

51.

"If there only ever had been intelligent beings, there would never have been material beings, for all the mental faculties are reducible to thinking and willing. But, being unable to understand how thought and will can act upon created beings, even less upon nothingness, I may suppose that none of it is true, unless Philoxenus can prove the opposite for me...

52.

"The intelligent being, according to him, is not at all a mode of corporeal being. There is no reason to believe that corporeal beings should be an effect of intelligent beings. It follows, then, from his belief and from my argument, that intelligent beings and corporeal beings are eternal, that these two substances make up the universe, and that the Universe is God.

53.

"Let Philoxenus carry on in that contemptuous tone which suits nobody, least of all a philosopher, and screech as he pleases: 'But you divinize butterflies, insects, flies, drops of water and every molecule of matter.' 'I divinize nothing,' I'd respond. 'If you can even begin to understand what I'm trying to do, you will see that the opposite is true: that I would like to banish all presumption, lies, and Gods from the world.'"

54.

Philoxenus, who had not expected such a vigorous attack from an enemy he had underestimated, was stunned. While he was collecting his thoughts, everyone's faces expressed that vile joy, born of that secret sort of jealousy which even the very philosophical souls are unable to escape. Philoxenus had triumphed so far, and all were glad to see him upset in this way, by an enemy he had treated in such a cavalier manner. I won't give you Philoxenus' reply: he had hardly begun when the sky was darkened; a thick cloud hid away the spectacle of nature, and we found ourselves in a dark night, which forced us to cut our dispute short and to send the decision back to those who had delegated us.

55.

Thus, we returned to the route of our alley. The tale of our voyage and our discussions were heard, the jury has retired to its chambers, and if a definitive judgment ever comes back, I'll be sure to let you know.

56.

Just know that, upon his return, Atheos found that his wife had been taken, his children's throats had been slit, and his house had been plundered. Many suspected the blindfolded man whom he had disputed with through the hedge, whom he had taught to despise the voice of conscience and the laws of society, when he could do it safely—this man was thought to have snuck away from the alley of thorns to commit this atrocity, since the absence of Atheos and the distance from all witnesses assured him of impunity. The most distressing part of the whole affair for poor Atheos was that he did was not free to complain; for, ultimately, the blind man had been a consistent in his beliefs.

THE ALLEY OF FLOWERS

He who forms to himself false Ideas of things,
And in Actions of a mix'd Nature
Is not able to distinguish that which is innocent,
From that which is criminal, is undoubtedly mad...
Horace, *Satires*, Book 2, Satire 3

1.

Although I neither go often nor stay long in the alley of flowers, I know it well enough by now to give you an idea of its situation and the thought of its residents. It is less an alley than an immense garden harboring everything that tickles the senses. Immense carpets of moss are followed by flower-strewn lawns, alongside turfs kept green by hundreds of streamlets. One finds somber woods where a thousand paths cross, labyrinths where people are happy to get lost, groves where people can hide, thickets offering places of concealment.

2.

They have carved out offices for various uses. In some you find tables decked with delicacies and buffets, spread with exquisite wines and liquors. In others there are gaming tables, cards, tokens, lotto tables: amusements enough to bankrupt oneself while having lots of fun.

3.

Here also gather some who pretend to think in a distracted manner, and who rarely speak their mind, overwhelming each other with politeness without knowing each other, often while hating each other. Exquisite parties are held, followed by even more delightful small suppers, which are spent cursing a woman, praising a stew, sharing well-prepared stories and mocking each other.

4.

Further along one finds large, bright, and shining salons. People laugh and cry in some; in others they are singing and dancing; elsewhere they engage in criticism, dissertation, disputation, shouting, most of time without knowing why.

5.

Here, Gallantry has established its empire. Love covets and coquetry simpers. Pleasure is all around; but cruel ennui is also everywhere—hiding right behind the pleasure. Lovers are common there; faithful ones are rare. Feelings are discussed all day long; but the heart is not even mentioned.

6.

I've said nothing so far about the more somber groves, where you find large canopies and soft sofas, you may well guess what these are for. They are changed so often, it is said that a single use wears them out.

7.

The public library is made up of everything that was ever written about love and its mysteries, from Anacreon to Marivaux. These are the archives of Cythera. The author of *Tanzaï et Néadarné* is in the stacks. Busts of the Queen of Navarre, Meursius, Boccaccio, and Fontaine are crowned with myrtles. People meditate on works like Marivaux's *Marianne*, Duclos's *Acajou*, and a thousand other trifles. Young boys read here, young girls devour the gallant stories of Father Saturnin. For here the general maxim is that the mind is never too young to be adorned and enlightened.

8.

However, people here are more interested in practice than theory, although it's accepted that the latter is not to be neglected. There are so many occasions in life where the vigilance of a mother is surprised, the jealousy of a spouse is fooled, and the suspicions of a lover are put to bed, that we really cannot fill our heads too early with good principles. In this way, in the alley of flowers people earn great praise in this regard. Moreover, they laugh much there, and the less they think the more they laugh. It is a whirlwind moving at an incredible speed. People only enjoy themselves there, that and disturbing others in their own enjoyments.

9.

All the travelers there walk backwards. Not really interested in the direction they're moving, they only want to finish the task in a pleasant way. Some of them bump up against the doors of the garrison, protesting that they have only been *en route* for a moment or so.

10.

What sets the tone with this whimsical people is a certain number of women, charming by their art and desire to please. One glories in her many admirers and wants the public to know all about it: another is happy to make many others happy; but their happiness must remain a secret. She will promise her favors to a thousand but only give it to one; another will only nurse the hopes of a single one, while she would not be cruel to a hundred others; all of this because of a secret that nobody keeps; for it's ridiculous to remain unaware of the adventures of a pretty woman, and it's fashionable to inflate numbers as necessary.

11.

Their washing-up session would be a general rendezvous for them, if the husbands were allowed in. Here the young, playful, and often enterprising folk gather, talking about everything without knowing anything, making every sort of trifle glitter, where they are skilled in seducing a pretty girl by getting rid of their rivals, passing from a serious discussion that they had started to the retelling of an adventure, or some circumstance which both keeps and rejects them, I know not how, onto an *ariette*, which they interrupt to speak politely, and conclude by profound reflections on a salon, a robe, a hoard from China, a nude by Clinchsted, a bowl from Saxony, a *pantine*[6] by Boucher, some trinket by Hébert, or a fine case by Juliette or Martin.

12.

Such is more or less the whole multitude who thoughtlessly wander in the alley of flowers. As they are all escapees from the alley of thorns, they never heard the voices of the Guides without quaking a little; so, for a certain part of the year the enchanted garden is almost vacant. Those who walk there do penance in the alley of thorns, from whence they waste not a moment in returning, only to go and repent again down the line.

13.

Their blindfold annoys them quite a bit; they spend a

---

[6] Defined as a "little feminine cardboard figure, whose parts were moved by pulling a string" (See Takeshi Matsumura. La pantine de Boucher dans La Promenade du sceptique de Diderot. FRACAS, Groupe de recherche sur la langue et la littérature françaises du centre et d'ailleurs (Tokyo), 2014, pp.5-9. <halshs-01081641>).

part of their life seeking means to escape this inconvenience. It is a kind of exercise in which they receive a few rays of light, but which soon vanish. Their eyes are not ready to see the full light of day; thus, they only leer from time to time, furtively. Nothing serious or consistent ever goes into those heads; the very word "system" confuses them. If they do believe in the Prince, they fail to draw any consequences that might interfere with their pleasures. A philosopher who reasons and who wants to wade too far into any subject is an annoying and tiresome creature to them. One day when I started to tell Themira of our sublime speculations, a gust of vapors came over her, from which she turned her languid eyes on me: "Oh, stop boring me," she said. "Think about having a good time, and give me one too." I obeyed, and she seemed as pleased with the man as she had been displeased with the philosopher.

14.

Their robe has got into a pitiful state; they apply soap to it every so often, but this operation is only temporary in its effect; it is only done for the sake of propriety. You would be forgiven for assuming that their principal objective is to decorate it with so many stains that you can't tell what its original color was. This is sure to displease the Prince, and despite the illusion of pleasure, there is something suspicious about this alley; for even though it is the most populous, and so many people fill the alleys, it begins to be depopulated by a third of the total, so that by the end there are only a few honest people left, those among us who go there for a quick recreation; for, to tell the truth, it is indeed a pleasant place, but you can't stay very long; it all goes to your head, and those who die there, die mad.

15.

Don't be surprised at the way time passes so quickly for them, or that they only leave reluctantly; as I already said, it is seductive to the eyes; everything there presents an enchanting aspect; the place is full of affability, cheerfulness, and good manners. Almost all the inhabitants could be taken for honorable and prudent people. It is experience alone that will disabuse us of our preconceptions, and this sometimes comes too late. I promise you, friend; I was the dupe of this world a hundred times before I really understood it, and learned to distrust it; and it was only after an infinity of deception, baseness, ingratitude, and betrayals that I managed to escape from the all-too-common stupidity of honest people, judging others by myself. As I believe you a very honest man who one day may be tempted to be as foolish as I was, I will sketch a few adventures for you; these will be useful for you, and may possibly make you laugh as well: listen then, and look at your own mastery, your own friends, and your own knowledge.

16.

Some time ago I found two people sitting in a grove far from the road; these were the courtier Agenor and the youth Phedima. Agenor, disillusioned with the court and world-weary, had, he said, renounced all honors: the caprices of the Prince and the injustices of the ministers had driven him away from a maelstrom, in which he had vainly tried to get ahead: in sum, he was now aware of the vanity of the powerful. Phedima, for her part a portrait of courtesy, had retained affection only for Agenor. Both had gone out from the world and had resolved to while away the rest of their days in love. I heard them cry out: "How happy we are! What happiness is like unto ours? Everything here breathes ease and freedom. O charming lands, what peace and innocence are not on offer here? Was the proud furnishing we have forsaken even worthy of our shadows? O golden chains, under which we groaned for so long, we only notice your weight when you are no longer wrapped around us! O brilliant yoke that people glory to bear, how fine it is to have shaken you off from our shoulders! Free from all discomfort, finally we swim in a sea of delights. Our pleasures, although simple, are no less intense for us. Amusements come and go, and ennui has never emptied its poison on them. Truly, those imperious duties, those forced attentions, and all the false respect will no longer be any bother. Reason has led us to here, and love alone has followed us—how different now from those days we sacrificed for ridiculous customs and bizarre tastes! If only this new era had begun sooner, and may it last forever! But why worry about a future, that may bring it to an end? Let's just enjoy ourselves, now."

17.

"My happiness," said Agenor to Phedima, "is written in your eyes: I will never leave my dear Phedima; no, never, I swear by those eyes. Exquisite solitude, you will settle all my desires; beds of flowers will I share with Phedima, you are the throne of love, and the throne of the king is less exquisite than you are to me."

18.

"My dear Agenor," responded Phedima, "nothing has ever touched me like the possession of your heart has done. Among all the courtiers, you alone have been pleased me and got me over my dislike for the quiet life. I have seen your fiery love, your faithfulness, your constancy, and I have left everything behind, but I have really left almost nothing behind. Tender Agenor, my dear and worthy friend, you alone are enough for me; I would live and die with you. This solitude was as dreadful to me then as it is joyful to me now; if these magical gardens should change into deserts, Phedima will see you there, Phedima will be happy there. May my own tenderness, faithfulness, my heart and the pleasures of a shared love, make up for the sacrifices you made for me! But, alas! These pleasures will end someday.... and with their loss, I will at least have the sweet consolation of feeling your hand closing my eyes, and of expiring between your arms."

19.

Friend, what do you expect happened next? Agenor, after having tasted the sweetest ecstasies upon the bosom of Phedima, went away from her, although briefly. He was to return after a moment to find her on their bed of flowers. But a carriage that had been waiting on him, carried him like lightning to the court. There he delayed a long time while pursuing his request for an important post. His credit, his intrigues, the intervention of his family, the bribes presented to the ministers and their mistresses, the upkeep of several women who had considered telling everything to Phedima, finally prevailed and obtained what he asked for, and letters arrived that announced his success an instant before embarking on the tender conversation with his mistress, which I related above.

20.

Agenor went away; and then a rival who had been waiting for his chance clambered out of a thicket he had been hiding in, and then took Agenor's place in the arms of Phedima. This newcomer had his reign like anyone else; she was overwhelmed with caresses, and this man had his own successors.

21.

You can see how true the love really is; now listen and judge for yourself how sincere friendships really are.

22.

Belisa was a close friend of Callista's; both were young, unmarried, adored by a thousand men, and decidedly on the side of pleasure. They were seen together at the ball, at the shows, at the promenades, at the opera; they were inseparable. They consulted each other on the more important matters. Belisa bought not one thread that Callista hadn't approved; Callista never went to see her jeweler unless accompanied by Belisa. What else can I say? Games, evenings out, suppers: with these two, all was in common.

23.

Crito was also a friend of Alcippus, they went all the way back: they shared the same tastes, the same talents, the same inclinations; mutual favors, good credit, common purse: the universe seemed to have destined their friendship and cemented it in place. Now, Crito was married, but Alcippus stayed single.

24.

Belisa and Crito knew each other. In a visit that Crito paid her, the conversation turned to the great issue of friendship. Feelings were shared, the subject was analyzed, each of them would testify to the other had an excessive sensibility and delicacy.

"It is an exquisite pleasure," said Belisa, "to be assured that one has friends, and that one deserves to have true ones, by a lively and tender interest that we feel for the things that affect them; but often we purchase this pleasure at great expense. As for me, I have felt only too keenly what it costs to have a heart tuned to the same high pitch as mine. What alarms! What concerns! What grief I have to share! But then, nobody is above such emotions..."

25.

"Ah! Madam," Crito responded, "will you ever tire of having such a beautiful soul? If I may quote myself, I will tell you that it is impossible for me, as for you, quite simply impossible, to refuse myself any feelings that I owe to my friends; but what will seem quite odd to you, I swear that I actually feel something sweet inside when my soul is rent by their concerns. Just between us, is it not essentially to lack feelings, if you are slow to feel tender at certain times?"

26.

"I never thought of it like that," Belisa cut in. "The truth is that the world is full of blackened hearts who cover up lies, wickedness, selfishness, treason, and a hundred other horrible faults, who on the outside present all possible probity, honor, and friendship. I fall into a bad mood, and I see a thousand things that almost make me suspicious of my best friends."

27.

"As for me, I don't worry about that sort of thing," said Crito. "I refrain from such excesses: I would rather be the dupe of a wretch than insult a friend. But to prevent both misfortunes, I study people profoundly before I ever bring them into my confidence, and I reject all those genial people who throw themselves into your arms but denigrate all sympathy through constant abuse thereof, who try to ingratiate themselves with you at all costs, although they know nothing about you, except that you're rich and prospering, or that you have a good chef, a lovely mistress, a young and pretty wife or daughter... What could be more common than to insinuate oneself into the house of a man in order to seduce his wife; and what could be worse! I don't mean to say that you should never invest your heart in your friendships, that you shouldn't attach yourself to anyone; it isn't even possible to live in the world at a certain tone without such diversions, but to try it on with your friend's wife—what a dark deed, what an ultimate depravity. The first is merely weak, and excusable; but this is pure evil, an unrivaled horror."

28.

"Forgive me", continued Belisa, "but I believe I can name a rival for it. An infamy that I detest just as much, which reveals a total absence of honor and respectability, is when a someone steals her friend's lover. Now that is diabolic; to do this you must first lack any trace of feeling or modesty—and yet we do know some people like that..."

29.

"So, madam", replied Crito. "You do know how many infamous people we constantly have dealings with."

30.

"Only too well", continued Belisa. "We see them, we receive them, we welcome them, and we just don't think much about it."

31.

"I feel the same way, madam", replied Crito. "I realize that people have better memories than you may think, and that such monsters are banished from all societies which are based on virtue, and where uprightness and candor are the rule; such societies do exist, after all."

32.

"I do agree with you", said Belisa; "I don't believe, for example, that you'll find any such people among us. Oh! What a great match we all make."

33.

"Since you have done me the favor of admitting me into your circle," replied Crito, "I must live up to such favors as come my way, especially yours, Madam, by a constant show of integrity. My feelings are well-reasoned. I act only on principle; by reason of which, principles are what I value. They are absolutely necessary; I judge anyone who lacks them unworthy of friendship."

34.

"That only stands to reason", added Belisa. "Oh, friends like you are too rare, and must be held tightly! Your feelings never surprise me. But I am always enchanted to find how comparable to my own they happen to be. Maybe I would be a little jealous if I did not know that virtues lose nothing by reproducing themselves, and that they are even increased when shared in discussions such as these."

35.

"In such frank and naïve communications, where well-born souls develop one another", said Crito, "in which consist the delights of friendship, which are only made for such as these."

36.

I would like very much to have your thoughts about such people. But I perceive that the adventure of Phedima and Agenor has put you on guard. You are distrustful of grand principles, and rightly so. Be brave, dear friend; if you are not amused, you may still benefit from it.

37.

Crito had hardly left Belisa, when Damis arrived. He was a rich young man with enviable features, and who had the hand of Callista promised to him. "You know", he told Belisa, "that charming Callista is to make me a happy man in the next two days. Everything has stopped cold; things will only progress if I buy her presents. You know it yourself; do I dare ask you to accompany me to Frenaye's place? My carriage is in your court."

38.

"Only too gladly," responded Belisa. They climbed into the carriage; making the journey, Belisa gave great praises to Callista at first:

"Oh! If only you knew her as I do!" she said to Damis. "She is easily the best little creature in the world."

"She would be perfect if only she were a little less lively," Damis interrupted.

"Come now, there are worse things than a little too much vivacity," replied Belisa. "But don't we all have our own failings: once again, she is very amiable; the unevenness in her character and these fierce moods that drive her most of the time, *à propos* of nothing, have not kept me from being her friend for a dozen years. I have overlooked these minutiae; but it would be great to get rid of her ditzy-ness; it does her no favors; for I love her with all my heart."

39.

"*Does her no favors*"! Interrupted Damis quite loudly,

“what are you talking about?”

“Oh”, continued Belisa, “I mean the way she can carry on, which is not entirely suitable to inspiring respect, has given more than hope to a few randy rascals.”

40.

“What am I hearing?” asked Damis, already overcome by clouds of jealousy. “*More than hope!* Would Callista toy with her innocence on me?”

41.

“That's not what I said”, continued Belisa. “But don't take my word for it: look, see for yourself. Committing oneself for life is an enterprise that deserves reflection.”

42.

“Madame”, added Damis, “if I have ever deserved your good-will, I ask you to swear to me that you won't leave me in the dark about things so central to my happiness. Can Callista have forgotten...?”

43.

“That's not what I said”, continued Belisa; “but she has been chatted up, and I am very surprised that you are not better informed...These early courtships are such terrible things," she added, feigning distraction. "But marriage often performs what neither reason nor all the brains in the world can do; for you must agree that Callista has both of these, in abundance."

44.

However, they arrived at la Frenaye's place: Belisa picked out the stones; Damis paid without arguing about the price, as his mind was elsewhere. His suspicions took over his heart, and his Callista unconsciously fell out of favor in his mind.

"Right," he told himself. "Something is going on under the surface here, since her best friend couldn't keep quiet." Prudence suggested he think more about it; but has jealousy ever taken the advice of prudence? They had hardly set foot in the carriage when Belisa annoyed him, put all her resources to work, ruthlessly tore Callista to shreds, advanced shamelessly, won Damis' favor, extracting promises that she at first pretended to reject, asked for the presents meant for Callista, and became the wife of her lover.

45.

While this perfidy was finishing up, Crito: yes, honest Crito, upon learning that Alcippus had gone into the countryside alone, took himself to the home of his friend, spent two or three nights in the arms of his wife, and left with her the next day to go and meet Alcippus, whom they overwhelmed with gentle caresses. Behold our good friends.

46.

I am committed to enlightening you about the value of all our knowledge, and I will keep my word.

47.

I was with Eros one day. You know him; you know the care, attention, money, and the efforts it has cost him to become an Ordinary Gentleman to the king, which he never obtained; how many doors he had to knock on; how many patrons he had, the protection that was promised to him, and the whole series of machinations that he set in motion. But you may not know how his dreams were spirited away at the last minute. Listen, and judge for yourself about the rest of those who dwell in the alley of flowers.

48.

Eros and I were walking one day; he was showing me all his favorite paths, when Narces accosted us. I judged from their gestures that they were close friends. "Okay," said Narces, after they traded a few compliments, "and your affairs, how does it stand?"

"It's basically a done deal," Eros responded. "All the pieces are in motion, and I expect to obtain my certificate tomorrow."

"How enchanting," Narces replied. "You are an admirable man for keeping your issues so quiet. I understand that you have the ear of the minister, and that the duchess Victoria has put in a word for you; but I will be honest and say that I always thought you'd fail. I saw too many obstacles in your way; how, I ask, did you ever get out of this labyrinth?"

49.

"Here's the truth," replied Eros ingeniously. "I had thought I had a good basis to seek a place that my father had occupied for a great long time, and which had only gone outside my family's possession because he died when I was too young to succeed him. I solicited, I spied out the occasions, and many were presented to me. I paid off the minister's footman and got a hearing with his master. I was assiduous in pressing my case, and I thought the affair basically over. I was there when Meostris died, and I learn that his post was actively sought after. I put myself forward too; I come, I go, and I find a man in the country who happens to be a second cousin of the Prince's nurse's chamber-maid: I leap headlong into that cascade; I win the nurse over; she takes up my cause, but she had already spoken for another. Rushing to cling to the side of my little Mona Lisa; I'd been told that she'd seen the minister. I run to her place, but all was lost; someone else had already been given the legacy: it was the dancer Asteria. Here, I told myself, is the right door to knock. This engagement is still fresh, and the minister will surely give the little actress the first thing she asks him: I must get this girl's attention."

50.

"What a sensible plan," said Narces. "And what came of that, then?"

51.

"Exactly what I expected," Eros continued. "A gentleman, one of my allies, went to find Asteria, offered her two hundred *louis*; she demanded four hundred, which I met; at that price I've won her to my cause: you see, my friend, to what lengths I went."

52.

"Ah!" responded Narces. "The place is yours: I embrace you, monsieur Gentleman of the Royal Chamber. You have definitely made it! ...Unless someone else outbids you."

53.

"That will never happen," said Eros. "You're the only one who knows, and I know how discreet you are..."

"You can count on that," replied Narces. "But tell me about your own discretion. Take my word for it, you really shouldn't go telling anyone else about this; by and large we don't know who we can trust, and all these people we think are our friends... you know what I mean... goodbye, I have promised to play lotto with that beautiful marquise I told you about, I must run."

54.

Narces disappeared with a good-bye. His advice was spot on, but unfortunately for Eros, he wasn't dealing with a more honest man: he should have kept his mouth shut with Narces himself. That traitor went straight to the courtesan, offered her six hundred louis, and defeated Eros.

55.

Such are the absurdities and vices of the alley of flowers; such are also its attractions. Its gates are not forbidden to us; for us, walking here can be a tonic against the cold air we breathe in our shade.

56.

One evening when I went out in search of rest and relaxation, I came upon some women who were leering at me through thin gossamer that covered their faces; I found them pretty, but not what I was after. I was particularly attracted to a brunette, upon whose large black eyes I furtively turned my own.

"In this fine place, with such a figure, you must be

making plenty of conquests," I told her...

"What! sir, move along, please," she responded. "I won't hear any more of your libertine propositions. The Prince is watching; my Guide can see me; I have a reputation to keep, a future to fear, a robe to keep spotless! Move along, please, or change your conversation."

57.

"But madam," I responded, "it is amazing that, with scruples like yours, you've found your way out of the thorny alley. Do I dare ask what you are about, coming down this one now?"

"To edify and convert, if possible," she said, smiling, "wicked men like you."

At that moment she noticed someone approaching her, she took up her modest and serious attitude again. She lowered her eyes, stopped talking, gave me a deep bow, then disappeared and left me in the middle of a group of crazed young girls who roared with laughter, irritated all passers-by, and made faces at everyone.

58.

It was among them that I thought to find the one who would have me; I mean, who would cheat me. I followed them; they soon gave me reason for hope.

"You see this tree?" One of them asked me. "All right,

since we're nearly at it..."

At the same time, she showed another one to a young man whom she had led quite a long way. When I came to the tree I had been shown, I was sent to a second one; from there to a third; finally to a grove whose large size was praised; and from there to another one supposed to be even bigger.

I then told myself, "I may well go on from tree to tree, and from grove to grove, following these mad-women as far as the garrison, without having obtained the least reward for my troubles." After this thought I quickly left them and addressed a young beauty who was, however, less charming. She was a blonde, but one of those blondes of which a philosopher must steer well clear. With a fine and slight build, she was still less symmetrical than she was alluring. In all my life I have never seen such lively colors, vivid skin, or prettier flesh. Beneath a simple hairstyle, covered by a straw hat lined in pink, her sparkling eyes breathed out her desires. Her words betrayed a cultivated mind; she loved argumentation: she was even good at it. The conversation was hardly begun between us when we fell on the subject of pleasure: such is the universal hypothesis and the inexhaustible material of the country.

59.

I soberly insisted that the Prince forbids such a thing, and that nature herself set bounds there. "I don't know your Prince," she told me. "But does this author and mover of all beings, good and wise as he is said to be, not give us as many pleasant feelings as painful ones? It is said he does nothing in vain; and what is the point of all our needs and desires, except to be satisfied?"

60.

I feebly suggested that maybe the Prince gave us these delights so that we had something to wrestle with, and he would have something to reward us for in the end.

She replied, "Would you really balance the present time which I can enjoy now, against that dubious future? It's obvious which the best bet is."

I hesitated; she noticed my confusion.

"Oh, are you serious?" she pursued. "You would have me unhappy now, in hope of some future happiness that may never come. Maybe if those laws, to which you would have me sacrifice my living body, were grounded in reason, but no! They are a random mish-mash of curiosities that seem like they were designed to make me deny my natural inclinations, and contradict the very author of my being. I am bound, I am irrevocably attached to a single man," she continued after a brief pause. "I forced him to beg for mercy; he recognized his weakness, without dropping his claims. He admitted defeat, but he could not endure any form of relief that would assure him of victory. When his forces failed him, what did he resort to? He hit me with all the prejudices in the book; but these are just another enemy that I must..." Cutting herself off at this point, she shot a passionate look at me; I offered my hand and led her into an enclosure in the greenery, where I proved to her how sound her arguments really were.

61.

We had thought ourselves safely distant from any witnesses when we noticed, through the foliage, a couple of prudes accompanied by two or three Guides who were staring at us. My lady blushed.

“What are you afraid of?” I asked under my breath. “Like you, these saints have, like you, brushed aside their prejudices in favor of their inclinations; in fact, they are really less offended by than jealous of your enjoyments. But, of course they won't be tempted to upset those who haven’t made out worse still than themselves. All we have to do is threaten to unmask their walking companions, and count on their discretion.”

Cephissa approved my expedient and smiled: I kissed her hand, and we went our separate ways, she onwards in search of new pleasures, me to go back to dreaming in our shady alley.

KEY TO THE SKEPTIC'S WALK

The first number indicates the section, the second the paragraph.

Aaron. 1:40

Abbots. 1:26.

Abraham. 1:38, 39.

Adam. 1:38.

Adventurers, 1:44.

Aeneid. 2:8.

Agenor, the name of a courtier. 3:16.

Alcmeon, the name of a Spinozist. 2:31, 36.

Alcyphron, a young skeptic, see the Preliminary Discourse.

Alexander of Hales. 1:27.

Alley of Chestnut-trees. 1:12, 16; 2:1, 2, 3, 4, etc.

Alley of Flowers, 1:13, 15; 3:1, 2, 3, etc.

Alley of Thorns. 1:11, 12, 13, etc.

Amazon (River), 1:1

Ambassadors, or Apostles and Evangelists. 1:44.

Anacreon. 3:7.

Anatomy. 2:47.

Ancona. 2:22

Anti-religious writers. 2:11

Ants, 2:36.

Apostates, see Deserters.

Apostles, see Ambassadors.

Archbishop, 1:25.

Aristos, name of author. Preliminary Discourse.

Ark. 1:40.

Armida. 2:23.

Army. 1:10.

Astronomy, 1:1

Atheism, see Atheists and Atheos.

Atheist. 1:3; 2, 5.

Atheos, the name of an atheist. 2:31, 32, 34, 36, 39, 44, 45, 46, 47, 56.

Atlas, 2:7.

Atticus, see the Preliminary Discourse.

Augustine, see Professor of rhetoric.

Augustus. 2:8.

Austrians, see the Preliminary Discourse

Auxiliary troops. Monks, 1:28, etc.

Auxiliary troops. Monks. 1:28, etc.

Aviaries. Convents for girls. 1:32

B... Dom. 3:7.

Babylon. 1:57.

Balance, the motto of the Pyrrhonians. 2:4.

Balm. Holy oils. 1:25.

Banner, a symbol of faith. 1:7,8,9,40,44,62,63

Baptism. 1:6.

Baptismal innocence, see white robe.

Barclay, see the Preliminary Discourse.

Battle cry of the skeptics, see Skeptics.

Beatific vision. 2:27.

Bees. 2:43, 47.

Belisa. A false friend. 3:21

Benedictines. 1:28, 29.

Bernardine, 1:28.

Bethlehem, 1:60.

Bishops, 1:15.

Black battalion. The Jesuits. 28,30

Black spot. Original sin, 1:38,40

Boasters. 2:9, 10, 31

Boccaccio. 3:7

Boucher, a painter. 3:11

Boxed-in people, 1:29,30

Bulls, see vellum.

Butchers or sacrificers. 1:40

Cafés. 3:4

Cages, see nunneries.

Calvin, see the Preliminary Discourse.

Canes. Grace, 1:45.

Capuchins, 1:28.

Carriers of water. Jewish priests. 1:40.

Carthusian monks and others, 1:28.

Casuists. Rigid. Relaxed. 1:31

Cervantes (Miguel), 1:65; 2, 22

Chestnut-trees. 2:1

Chevaux de frise. 1:30.

Christ. 1:43, etc.

Christianity. 1:48, etc.

Christians, see Christ and Christianity, or the Alley of Thorns, 1:4.

Cicero, see the Preliminary Discourse.

Cinna. 2:8.

Circumcision, 1:7, 40.

Circumincession. 1:44.

Cleobulus. Philosopher retired from the world, see the Preliminary Discourse.

Clinchsted. Painter.

Cobbler, Former Gentleman. Paul, 1:44.

Cochin, see Preliminary Discourse.

Code. Old and New Testaments. 1:4, 9, 33, 34, 36, 37, etc.; 2:19.

Colonel, see Christ.

Comedy. 3:4.

Commentators. 2:46.

Communion, see Eucharist and transubstantiation.

Compostella. 2:23.

Confessors, see enclosed-ones, 1:29.

Consubstantiation, see the Preliminary Discourse.

Convents, see auxiliaries, cages, aviaries.

Corpus callosum. 2:27.

Cowards. Bad Christians. 1:8.

Crébillon (junior). 3:7.

Crito, false friend. 3:9.3.

Crow's beak cane. A staff. 1:25.

Crutches. 1:45.

Cuzco. 2:24.

Cybele, 1:25.

Cytherus. 3:7.

Damis, the name of a Pyrrhonist. 2:31, 38.

Decalogue. 1:40.

Degreasers. Confessors. Casuists. 1:47.

Deists, 1:3; 2:6.

Delphi. 1:40.

Deluge. 1:38.

Deserters. Apostates, 1:8, 9.

Devil, see Magician.

Devotees, see Alley of Thorns.

Diphilus, the name of a skeptic. 2:31, 39.

Directors of nuns. 1:32

Disciples of Jesus Christ, see the Preliminary Discourse.

Discussion between a false friend and a young man. 3:37.

Discussion between a false male friend and a false female friend. 3:24.

Discussion between a pagan philosopher and Christian. 1:49.

Discussion between a philosopher and a courtesan. 3:59.

Discussion between an atheist and a Christian, 1:14.

Discussion between philosophers. 2:32

Discussion between two false lovers. 3:16.

Discussion of the author and philosopher of his friends, see the Preliminary
Discourse.

Discussion of two kinds of knowledge of the world. 3:47.

Dispensations, see Soap, Vellum.

Distinct troops. Doctors, 1:27.

Down slippers. 1:31

Duclos. 3:7.

Dulcinea. 2:22

Dull lantern. Beatific vision. 2:27.

Dutchmen, see the Preliminary Discourse.

Easter. 1:40.

Ecclesiastical hierarchy, see Staff.

Ecclesiastical history, see the Preliminary Discourse.

Egotistical. 2:8.

Englishmen, see the Preliminary Discourse.

Epaminondas. 1:59.

Eros, the name of a good man fooled. 3:47.

Eucharist. 1:44,

Eve. 1:38.

Executioners, see Inquisitors.

Existence of God, 1:3; 2:14, etc.

Kaleidoscope, 1:9.

Faith, see banner, 1:7, 8, 9, etc.

Farmer. Jethro. 1:35.

Favorites of the vice-regent, or friends of Roman Court. 1:24.

Fishermen, see cowards.

Fishmonger, Peter. 1:44, 45.

Flirts. 3:57, 58.

Flowers (Alley of). 3:1

Fontenoy (day of), see the Preliminary Discourse.

Frederick, King of Prussia, see the Preliminary Discourse.

Frenaye, a jeweler. 3:37, 44.

Freston. 1:65.

Friar John (Character from Rabelais) 1:21

Friendships. 3:21

Fullers. Degreasers. Confessors. Casuists. Boxed-in ones. 1:47.

Future rewards. 2:27.

Future torments. 1:63.

Gallant women. 3:10, 58.

Garrison, see rendezvous.

Gendron. 2:22

General officers. Patriarchs and prophets, 1:9

General rendezvous. The other world. 1:5,10

Geographer. 1:2

Geography. 1:1

Geryon. 1:44

Glasses, 1:1

Godfathers. 1:6

Godmother. 1:6

Government, see **Martial**; also see the Preliminary Discourse.

Governors. Archbishops, 1:25.

Graces, see canes, 1:45.

Guides. Priests. 1:10, 20, 21, 22, 23, 62

Hardouin. 2:20.

Hebert. 3:11

Hell. 1:65.

Hereditary benefices. 1:41,

Heroes, see martyrs.

Holy water, 1:64.

Horace, 1., 2., 3. Also quoted on the frontispiece and the Preliminary Discourse.

Hypostasis, see the Preliminary Discourse.

Hypostatic union, see the Preliminary Discourse.

Idumea, see Judea. 1:56.

Illuminative life, etc. 2:21

Incarnation, see the Preliminary Discourse.

Inquisition. 1:28.

Inquisitors. 1:28.

Inspired books, see deists, 1:4.

Inspired men. 1:4.

Instituted signs, 1:7.

Intolerance, see the Preliminary Discourse.

Isaac. 1:59.

Itinerant serinettes, or directors of nunneries. 1:32

Jacob, 1:39.

Jansenists, 1:31

Japhet of Armenia (Dom). 1:25.

Jerusalem. 1:56.

Jesuits. 1:28, 29.

Jesus Christ, see Christ.

Jethro. 1:35.

Jews. 1:4, 42, 47, etc.

John Huss, see the Preliminary Discourse.

John, the Apostle, 1:59.

Jonathan. 1:59.

Joppa. 1:56.

Joseph, the patriarch. 1:39.

Josephus, a historian. 1:59.

Judas, 1:59.

Juliette. 3:11

Junior officers. Archbishops. Bishops. 1:15, 25.

Justus of Tiberias. 1:58.

Knowledge of the world, see Eros.

La Fontaine. 3:7.

Lapland. 1:1

Libertines. 2:9, 10.

Lord of the parish, see Pharaoh.

Lotto. 3:3.

Louis, 1:1, see also the Preliminary Discourse.

Loves. 3:16.

Luther, see the Preliminary Discourse.

Machiavelli, see the Preliminary Discourse.

Madrid. 2:24.

Magician. Devil. 1:64.

Mahogany. 3:7.

Manuscript cited, see the discussion of the pagan philosopher and the Christian.

Marauders. 1:38

Marianne. 3:7.

Marivaux. 3:7.

Mark. 1:54,57

Martial. Inquisition. Clergy. 2:13

Martin. A varnisher. 3:11

Martyrs. 1:48

Marvelous dance, 1:44

Mass, see Eucharist or Transubstantiation.

Massacre of innocents. 1:60

Matadors. Princes. 1:24

Médoc (Duke of). 1:65

Menippus. 1:48

Meostris, see Eros.

Meursius. 3:7

Milton. 1:65

Mine. 1:4

Miracles. 1:48

Missionaries. 1:28

Miter. 1:25

Monasteries for girls. 1:32

Monks, 1:28,29

Montaigne, see the Preliminary Discourse. 2:4

Montesquieu, see the Preliminary Discourse.

Mortification. 2:21,22

Moses, see Shepherd, Old and New Testaments.

Muslims, see the Preliminary Discourse.

Mysteries, 1:9.

Narces. A false man. 3. to 7.

Navarre (Queen of). 3:7.

Navigation. 1:1

Nerestor, the name of a skeptic. 2:31,38.

Newton. 1:1

Noah. 1:38.

Noon. 1:1

North. 1:1

Nuns. 1:32

Oils, see balm, 1:25.

Old Academy. 2:1

Old and New Testaments, 1:4, 40.

Opera. 3:4.

Opinions, see the discussion of philosophers and the Alley of Chestnut-trees.

Oribasius, the name of a Spinozist. 2:31, 47, 48.

Original sin, 1:38

Pancakes. 1:40

Parliaments. 1:24

Partisans. 2:11

Passage through the Red Sea. 1:35

Patriarchs, see general officers.

Paul, cobbler, see Former gentleman.

Pelopidas. 1:59

Pendulum. 1:33

People of God. 1:35

Peru. 1:1

Peter, see Fishmonger.

Pharaoh. 1:38

Phedima, name of a courtesan. 3:18

Philo. 1:5f.

Philosophers. 2:1

Philosophical reflections, see the Preliminary Discourse.

Philosophical retirement, see the Preliminary Discourse.

Philosophy. 2:1

Philoxenus, the name of a deist. 2:31, 35, 38, 39, 40, 43, 45, etc.

Pilgrims. 1:29

Philosophical inscription, see the Preliminary Discourse.

Pindar. 1:59

Pineal gland. 2:27

Pitfalls. 1:31

Plagues of Egypt. 1:35

Plato, see the Preliminary Discourse.

Poles. 2:31

Preachers. 1:29

Predecessors. First popes. 1:24

Predestination, see the Preliminary Discourse.

Predilection, 1:38

Prejudices of the Public (a book), see the Preliminary Discourse.

Prescriptions. 1:30

Priests, see Guides. 1:20

Privileged. Ancient and modern. 1:4,38

Professor of rhetoric. St. Augustine, 1:45

Promised Land, 1:42

Prophets, see general officers.

Protestant. 1:44

Provost, see Inquisitor. 1:28

Prudes. 3:56

Psalms, 1:18

Puppets, see Boucher, a painter.

Pyrrho. 2:4

Pyrrhonians. 2:4

Quadrant, 1:1

Quietists. 1:29

Quinze-vignt (a hospital for ophthalmology in Paris), 2:22,30

Rabelais quoted. 1:21

Real Presence. 1:9

Reason advanced. 1:1

Recruiters. 1:10

Recruits, peculiar. 1:26

Religion, see the Preliminary Discourse.

Residence of the Prince, 1:5

Respectable prejudices, see the Preliminary Discourse.

Resurrection. 1:45,65

Roads, 1:11

Romans. 1:7,28

Rome. 1:56; 2:23

Ruler in Chief. God: 1:3

Sabbath. 1:40

Sables. 1:1

Sacred writers, 1:34

Salad. 1:40

Sancho. 2:22

Saracens. 1:28.

Saturninus, see B.... (Dom)

Saxony (the Marshal of), see the Preliminary Discourse.

Secretaries. Sacred authors.

Self-esteem. 2:21,28

Servandoni. 2:23

Sex. Advantage of sex. 1:7

Shepherd. Old shepherd or Moses. 1:35, 36, etc.

Sibyl. 1:40

Sign of the Cross, see symbolic gesture.

Silkworms. 2:43

Sipahis, 1:26

Skeptics, 1:3; 2:10

Slaps. 1:24

Soap. Absolution, dispensations, etc. 1:24,25

Socinus, see the Preliminary Discourse

Socrates, see the Preliminary Discourse

Soldierly duties, see Soldier or White robe

Soldiers, 1:6, 8, 16, 17, etc.

Songs. Psalms. 1:18

Spinoza. 2:7

Spinozists. 2:7

Staff: Clergy. 1:23

Star, see the Preliminary Discourse.

Sub-Rulers, etc. Bishops. 1:25

Sub-Rulers. 3:11

Swift, see the Preliminary Discourse

Symbolic gesture. Sign of the Cross, 1:64

Tables of the Law, see Decalogue

Tanzai. 3.7

Thebans. 1:56

Theologians, see Guides, and the Preliminary Discourse

Theudas. 1:59

Thorns, 1:1, 2, etc.

Timare. 1:20

Tripod. 1:40

Tocane. 2:10

Toilet. 3:11

Tolerance, see the Preliminary Discourse.

Torno (river), 1:1

Transubstantiation, see the Preliminary Discourse, 1:44

Trinity, see the Preliminary Discourse, 1:44

Truth. A watch-word. 2:31

Turks. 1:26

Uniform. 1:7

Urania (Voltaire's poem). 2:1

Vellum. Bulls, briefs, indulgences, etc. 1:44,45

Velvet mittens. 1:31

Vicars. 1:26

Vice-regent. Pope. 1:24, etc.

Virgil. 2:8, 47

Voltaire (de), see the Preliminary Discourse.

Watch-word. 1:9; 2:31

Watch. 2:33

White cassock, or white robe, a symbol of baptismal innocence. 1:7

White robe, symbol of innocence. 1:7, etc., 40,44,63

Woolston, see the Preliminary Discourse

World, see the discussion of the philosophers. 1:34

Worms. 2:36

Xanthus, an atheist. 2:31

Zenith. 2:32

Zenocles, a Pyrrhonian. 2:31,41,42

Made in the USA
Columbia, SC
09 September 2018